MATT TALBOT
AND HIS TIMES

BY

MARY PURCELL

With a Foreword by

HIS GRACE THE MOST REV. DERMOT RYAN, D.D.
Archbishop of Dublin, Primate of Ireland.

Revised Edition

FRANCISCAN HERALD PRESS
1434 WEST 51st STREET ● CHICAGO, 60609

Matt Talbot and His Times by Mary Purcell. American edition published by special arrangements with the author and publisher C. Goodlife Neale Ltd., Dublin, Ireland. Copyright © 1977, Franciscan Herald Press, 1434 West 51st Street, Chicago, Illinois 60609.

Library of Congress in Publication Data:

Purcell, Mary, 1906 -
    Matt Talbot and his times.

    1.   Talbot, Matthew, 1856-1925. 2.   Catholics in Dublin—Biography. 3.   Dublin—Biography. I. Title.
BX4605.T27P8   1977   282'.092'4 [B]   77-3556
ISBN 0-8199-0657-3

NIHIL OBSTAT:
    Michael O'Connell,
    Censor Theol Deput.

IMPRIMI POTEST:
    +Dermitius,
    Archiep. Dublinen., Hiberniae Primas

Dublini, die 26 Novembris, anno 1976.

Matt Talbot's First Grave in Glasnevin

Although no pomp attended him,
   The stream's procession all day long
   Files past him, and the stately throng
Of surpliced clouds, from rim to rim
   Of heaven, pass him, and the song
Of seabirds, where dim islands loom,
Makes requiem above his tomb.

And though no canopy was spread
   Above his wrinkled corpse, each night
   A swift angelic acolyte
Enkindles stars above his head;
   And reverentially and light
The cool asperges of the rain
Falls on that form, once hot with pain.

                —Liam Brophy.

Matt Talbot

INTRODUCTION

It is in the last scene of a much talked of film. Whiskey glass in hand, the chronic alcoholic looks languidly at the liquor. There is indecision in his face, changing suddenly to desperate determination. I forget: Was it the match or the cigarette that he scrunched into the glass? No matter. The point is that he made a decision: No more drink!

That gesture left me unconvinced. If the picture had continued, would he be doing the same tomorrow, and the next day, and the next? Perhaps.

Transfer that alcoholic back about one hundred years, place him in a Dublin bar, and you have a picture of Matt Talbot as he was rounding out his twenties. Already his paycheck was blown in for drink. His galloping thirst was too far ahead of him. His paycheck was far too small to last out the week. By that time he had to mooch drinks from his pals. But they got tired of giving. Then one evening they gave him the bum's rush—refused to offer him a drink. That hurt!

But it was a healing cut. It was in that flash of wounded pride that the deep loneliness of Matt's soul suddenly overwhelmed him. He knew now what a fool he had been. Bending the knees of his soul to but one god—drink. His whole mind's march but to one thing —drink. His work's wages wasted on one object—drink. His whole character formed by one master—drink.

Furiously he bent every energy into dousing a cigarette into the thing he wanted most. Then and there he made up his mind to quit drinking. And he did quit! It was never again the "same old story." Part II of his life began that evening, a life written in simple saintliness.

Matt Talbot was born in Dublin Ireland in 1856. His parents were poor. The children had to work early. At twelve Matt was errand boy for a wine merchant; at thirteen he came home drunk—on wine. He was removed, by his father, to work on the docks; he came home drunk again—on whiskey. At seventeen he became a bricklayer, a willing, whistling worker but an incorrigible toper. His week's wages were handed over in lump to the bartender, who then proceeded to dole out drink to the dawdling drunk. By the middle of the week he was through his money and became then, I suppose, a kind of barfly, taking or begging a shot from anyone who would stand him one.

He did everything to get his drink, even putting his shoes in hock. I used to think such things were a little far-fetched until recently, through some circumstance, I was standing in a We-Buy-and-Sell-Used Clothing shop on West Madison Street, Chicago. One of the many unfortunates of that neighborhood came in out of the zero weather, slowly took off his cap, and asked Max, the owner, what he would give him for it. They settled for fifty cents. Said Max to me: "He's just got to have his booze." The man ran hatless out of the shop to the corner tavern.

By the time Matt was twenty-eight a rigid routine held him down to his loose life. Impossible for him ever to break that bond, it seemed. His mother was broken-hearted. For fifteen years he had gone on that way.

Then came the incident related above. Matt made up his mind slowly, deliberately, as methodically as a machine that cannot turn back its gears. He would take the pledge. His mother tearfully sent him off "in God's name," calling after him "not to take it unless you are going to keep it." Poor woman! No doubt, there had been good resolutions before.

But now the rough firmness in Matt's character stood stern; there was a clean cleavage in this decision of his life. That evening he took the pledge, made his confession (he had neglected confession for the past three years), and with his mother's words—"God give you strength to keep it"—in his ears, he began his new life.

A certain shrewd strategy accompanied Matt's change of heart. He did not take the pledge flatly, for good. He took it twice for three months. That seemed manageable; he could hold out that long! Then he renewed it for a year. Finally, for life. Gauge the agonies Matt must have gone through during those first miserable months when his whole physical bent was toward drink!

But he sought strength where he knew it could not fail: in prayer and in the Holy Eucharist. He had haunted the bars of Dublin; now he was seen huddled in the back of Dublin's churches. "O Virgin," he kept saying, "I ask only three things—the grace of God, the presence of God, the benediction of God," Or that other prayer. "O most sweet Jesus, mortify within me all that is bad—make it die."

He just had to pray. During those first months he hung on to his resolution by his eyebrows, half-despairingly aware that once the three months were up, he would simply fall in again where he had left off. But prayer won out. He prayed for the grace of prayer and got it in abundance. His hunger for it slowly defeated his hankering for liquor.

It was six years later, 1890, that Matt was invested

in the Third Order Secular at the Church of Adam and Eve, Merchants Quay, Dublin; and he made his profession in October, the following year. In the Third Order of St. Francis and its ideal of penitential love he found the training ground for holiness.

He was usually to bed by 10:30. At 2:00 A.M. he rose to pray. After a short nap sometimes, he dressed definitely at 4:00, prayed until shortly before 5:00, and knelt on the church steps for half an hour until the sexton opened the doors. Mass was at 6:15. He returned home for breakfast. Then off to work at 7:45. At 6:00 P.M. he left the lumberyard, stopped in church to say the Angelus, then went home for his evening meal. After supper he either went to devotions or to a meeting in one of the societies to which he belonged. Often he sat up and read, or visited the sick.

Such was the framework of his day. His prayer was practically continuous. His bed were unplaned boards, a block of wood his pillow. His fasts were rigorous; for nine months of the year he ate no meat. Rarely did he use butter or milk. On working days his midday meal was a slice of bread and a little weak tea. Surprisingly enough, when he ate out, he would take as much as anyone else.

All of that was not undertaken at a blow. It was a gradual thing. It grew as the light and strength of grace was received. For the last fourteen years of his life he wore chains around both his waist and his arms and legs. We shrink at the suggestion of it. Not for us, we think. Yet there is an equivalent that each of us must bear. More of that below.

In 1923, when Matt was sixty-seven, his heart began

to tap weakly. He was taken, twice that year, to Mater Misericordiae Hospital. It was like him to take off his chains before entering; that secret was between himself and God. The Anointing of the Sick was administered. But he grew well enough to leave the hospital.

All that he had discontinued, was now resumed: prayer, fasts, chains. In April 1925 he even went back to his work in the lumberyard. But people could not help seeing that "Matt was not long for this world."

On June 7, Trinity Sunday, he went to an early Mass, came home for breakfast, and set out again for St. Savior's. Near the church he fell. A woman ran across to him, but he died without speaking. A bystander made the sign of the Cross over him with a crucifix, and a priest hurried to the scene.

At the mortuary the real Matt Talbot was at last found out. They found his chains on him, bedded in many places in the flesh. With that the rest of his life became clear. Much deeper in holiness was this man than indicated in the formula the men had for him: "Everyone loves Matt—he don't care for money." He had kept his life hidden with Christ in God. He had lived among his fellow men as if behind a monastery wall. No one suspected that in that thin shadow of a man the heart of a saint was beating.

In that same year a girl who had lived behind the walls of Carmel, was canonized—St. Therese of Lisieux. Death revealed her as a saint, as it revealed Matt Talbot.

On the feast of Corpus Christi, clothed in his Franciscan Tertiary habit, Matt was buried with his chains in Glasnevin Cemetery.

Roughly, that is Matt Talbot's life looked at from without. Featureless. Drab. Like the dull gray of a light bulb. You must turn on the switch, to see the bulb transmuted into a glowing mass. We must see Matt in his spiritual, religious life to appreciate his greatness. It was by that nondescript way of life that he made himself a saint—not in spite of it. We may not overlook the more than forty years after his pledge. During that long martyrdom Matt sanctified himself simply by being a model day laborer in a lumberyard, a union laborer at that. Nothing ever happened to him. He happened to those about him, as a light happens to a dark room.

We have suggested briefly what went on in Matt's innermost soul. But we cannot omit the picture others had of him, particularly his fellow workmen. We have no satisfactory photograph of Matt Talbot, but from descriptions we know that he was thin but erect, always very neat, never a suggestion of slovenliness or slouch.

Further, he was no timid Casper Milquetoast, for he dominated his environment by sheer force of character. To his fellow laborers he was kindly, considerate, generous in lending money, very direct in speech where direct speech was called for, capable then even of the heat of anger. Lying ceased, for he hated it. Profanity sloughed slowly from the lumberyard; he talked up ruthlessly on this matter, and if talk was not enough, he produced a crucifix and spoke bluntly of Christ dying on the Cross.

I have mentioned that the men said commonly Matt had no use for money. But he had a use for it: he gave almost all of it to charities and to the missions, helping God's kingdom to come. He sympathized fully with his fellow workers, was outspoken when injustice was evident, joined them passively in a strike, but he would not tolerate picketing; as he viewed it, for a worker to deprive another of the means of livelihood was a greater injustice than for an employer to pay inadequate wages.

He was not a man to start "religious talk." Neither was there any hint of fanaticism or pharisaism about him. Men hate that. Matt liked a good joke, laughed and sang with the others. Only they sensed that in Matt there was something different; he was a "better man than they."

Matt Talbot is a man close to us, as close as a friend whom we call by his clipped first name. That "Matt" puts the man at our elbow. Could the official prayer of the Church (for the Catholic press has been carrying notices about his cause of beatification) leave the homely, intimate Matt? The workingman today needs him close at hand.

The whole character of Matt Talbot is such that the ordinary workingman instinctively and admiringly would call him "a great fellow." If that sounds queer, Matt's own language was no different. Once, when referring to two of his models in the life of penance and reparation, St. Mary Magdalene and St. Mary of Egypt, he spoke of them as "those great girls." In any case, by "great" we mean here people who put energy into their Catholic life, men and women who are true to their convictions, courageously uncompromising, firm in the faith they live.

Keeping that idea of greatness in mind, we shall better understand the Holy Father's allocution of the last week in January 1947. "Today we require," he said, "the greatness of Christianity lived in its fulness with persevering constancy." Insisting that this is the greatest crisis the Church has gone through since her infancy, the Holy Father called on the faithful to enroll in a gigantic order of the laity, "a valorous array of men and women living in the world," taking up the role of St. John the Baptist to "prepare the way of the Lord in our own and our neighbor's life."

The greatness of Christianity lived in its fulness—what, really, does the Holy Father mean? We can begin by keeping our mind on Matt Talbot; he is the impressive action picture of what the Holy Father wants of us in this age of crisis. He was an example, a man whom others instinctively, if unconsciously, imitate.

"A reasoned, scientific exposition of our faith is not enough," the Pope goes on to say. "Neither is the Christian life lived because of conventional habit. Today we require the greatness of Christianity." He describes it: "Firmness in faith, courage to observe totally the law of God and of the Church—a thing that requires self-control, effort, sometimes heroism, and always a refusal to compromise. Zeal—ardent zeal." Like Matt Talbot's, our life in the words of the Pope ought to be "not a matter of persuasive words, but of greatness." Great fellows—like Matt Talbot's "great girls."

The greatness of Christianity lived with persevering constancy. "It is constancy God wants," was Matt's frequent expression.

One of the hardest parts of Matt's life for us to keep a steady gaze on, are precisely those chains he wore. But we dare not overlook them even if we have not the grace to wear them, for they are a symbol of what the Holy Father wants.

The chains denote a penitential state, unrelaxed pressure brought to bear on our duty, continually and courageously. None of us can escape the equivalent of those chains if we are to be our Lord's disciples. Only a daily cross makes us worthy of him—up to his level. Each of us knows what pressure points and pain pricks we are shirking most, though we ought not and may not shy from them. Matt at our elbow is our example of constancy in Christian greatness.

Again let us stop. Today we need "a gigantic order of the laity," dedicated to the greatness of Christianity, in firm faith, self-control, courage, zeal!

The Holy Father lays down a rule for us to follow in this crisis, as a counter offensive. Generally, "our rule, in personal life and in social relations, is the admonition of Christ: If any man will come after me, let him take up his cross and follow me." "Your counter offensive is through good example, a prayerful, self-sacrificing life, and vigorous profession of the Faith."

Where is that order of laity? Where find such a rule of life? Matt Talbot was buried in the habit of the Third Order of St. Francis. The twofold rule of penance in personal life and in social relations which Matt Talbot carved out so accurately, is precisely the aim of the Third Order of Penance.

The mission of the Third Order is none other than that twofold rule the Holy Father insists on: reforming the heart of the individual, and through the individual sanctifying the whole of society by carrying the cross after Christ.

There is nothing extraordinary about the Third Order rule, no more than what the Pope calls for: good example, a prayerful, self-sacrificing life, and vigorous profession of the Faith.

Thus Matt Talbot's life, like that of another John the Baptist, points the way for the men and women of this century. His life is epitomized in the names he chose when he entered the Third Order—Joseph, Francis. Joseph, the model of workmen, teaching them that work is service to the King. Francis, gallantly mirroring Christ and showing men and women the way to follow Christ.

—Mark Hegener O.F.M.

MATT TALBOT'S PHOTO
(Frontispiece)

From *Osservatore Romano,* February 17, 1977 (English Edition) we reprint the following story about the photograph of Matt Talbot which serves as the frontispiece of this book. It was written by Father Leo Dolan, pastor of St. Leo Church in St. Paul, Minnesota.

"You'll never see a photo of Matt Talbot. He was always too poor to have one taken." Thus wrote the late Eddie Doherty, star Chicago reporter of 40 years ago, in his biography of the recovered Dublin alcoholic whom Pope Paul VI says he hopes to beatify.

Referring to a formal studio portrait, Doherty was right. Talbot was never able to afford one. And, if one had been offered free, he would have declined out of his strong sense of humility.

Yet today, we have a photograph of Matt Talbot. And the way it was discovered and reproduced makes an interesting tale.

When I got interested in Matt Talbot some years ago, I looked around for a likeness of the man who was then emerging as a hero for people struggling with the disease of alcoholism. The only thing I found was an imaginative painting done by an artist who had never seen Talbot, and it was done in 1935, ten years after his death. It was like one of those composite portraits done by police experts in an effort to identify a criminal. No one could be sure how exact it was.

This portrait, incidentally, still hangs in the corridor of the Jesuit Church on Gardiner St. in Dublin, where Talbot often went to Mass.

Sometime later, I met an old man in Dublin named Paddy Laird who had worked with Talbot in a lumberyard when they were both young.

I asked him what Talbot looked like, and we talked for a while about the saintly recovered alcoholic who had been Laird's good friend.

Suddenly he said, "Father, I think there may be a picture of him. When we both worked for the T. and C. Martin Co., they had a picture taken of the inside of the furniture factory, and I think Matt was in a group in the background."

He went off and returned with an ancient photograph. "There he is," he exclaimed, pointing to one figure in the background.

I asked, somewhat sceptically, if he was sure, and, to prove his point, he ticked off the names of several other men in the group.

The figure identified as Talbot was not very clear. It looked as though he had moved slightly just as the camera snapped, and the resulting picture was slightly fuzzy. To compound this difficulty, the man was standing in the shadow of a wooden post. To make matters even worse, the photograph I held was then about 60 years old.

I suddenly recalled a tour of the headquarters of Control Data Company in Minneapolis several weeks previously. They showed me their advanced techniques for the enlargement and clarification of aerial photography. Could these same techniques bring a recognizable likeness out of the fuzzy old photo, I wondered?

Paddy Laird gave me the picture to take back to the States and try.

My friends at Control Data worked hard on this project. It was by far their most unusual task, enlarging the photo of a prospective saint rather than that of some defence target.

The resulting photograph was a great tribute to the skill of the people at Control Data. When it was shown around to many who knew Matt Talbot, it was authenticated by all without exception.

The first copy now hangs in the Church of Our Lady of Lourdes in Dublin where Talbot is buried. Another copy was given to Pope Paul VI on May 11, 1974, when he received members of the Calix Society in audience.

The real Matt Talbot revealed in the photo has a much more interesting face than the one on the oil painting. This is the face of a real man, someone that one would have liked to know.

(Frontispiece in this edition is a reconstructed composite of different angle shots of the original picture described in this article taken by Soltis Photographers.)

PREFACE

A prophet is not received in his own country. Are these words true of Matt Talbot? We honour Martin de Porres, the coloured saint; we honour St Jude for his gifts, St Francis Xavier for his miracles of grace. Our devotions take us all over the spiritual world. Yet here amid the once proud Georgian houses of Dublin—serving the cargo boats that ploughed their way up the Liffey, kneeling at daily Mass as many a Dubliner still does—lived a man in whom the light of Christ shone forth.

Many know of him as a reformed drunkard whose excesses of penance drove him to wear chains. A bit of an oddity, they would say. But with God's grace and the prayers of our people that unique man will one day, please God, take his place in the company of the Church's saints. That will come about through the informed devotion of the Irish people and of workers everywhere. We need to know about Matt Talbot. We need to be devoted to him. We need to imitate him. Mary Purcell's book will help us.

Miss Purcell's work as a biographer has taken her through half the countries of Europe and she has the ability to capture the atmosphere of 16th century Spain as of 17th century France. She is utterly and effortlessly at home in the Dublin of the turn of the century, making it live again for us with its over-crowded tenements, its hunger during the 1913 lock-out, its aristocrats aloof in the grandeur of Merrion and Mountjoy Squares. But she brings to life in a special way the homely and moving story of a Dublin workman whose conversion was in the great tradition of Irish spirituality, rugged and austere yet gentle and devoted, with all the extravagant devotedness of a lover.

4

Matt Talbot has a lesson, a message we all need to learn. It is time we began.

For the child, idling precious time away through frequent absences from school, Matt's message lies in the single curt comment in an old school roll-book—"a mitcher". Matt spent many painful hours trying to recover time lost in reading and writing classes. In the end he never really made it up. The range of his reading, though wide, was limited by this drawback; and, more important still, because writing was difficult for him, the inner depths of his prayer life remain hidden. That is a tragedy.

For the alcoholic, smitten with remorse and self-loathing, Matt Talbot has a message. The first three months "dry" were, he said, the hardest of all his life. Nothing—not even the severe fasts and the nights spent in prayer during the forty years that followed his conversion—was more difficult. Prayer, especially prayer to Our Lady, gave him strength, determination and the will to persevere.

The laity are encouraged today to read the Bible; for them Matt has a message. It was an astonishing achievement for an almost illiterate man to pore successfully and fruitfully over the Book of Deuteronomy, the Gospel of St John and the Epistles of St Paul. Matt Talbot's experience says that the Bible is truly a book for Everyman once he has been touched by the grace of the Holy Spirit.

For people who find themselves lonely, isolated, either in a depopulated countryside or in the new estates developing around our cities and towns, Matt has a message. We find it in the courtesy and delicacy of his neighbourliness and also in his care and love for the members of his family, some of whom at times must have seemed rather unlovable.

At this time, when we are trying to deepen our devotion for the sacrament of Penance, Matt Talbot's devotion to Confession is striking. The candid and beneficial discussions he had with his spiritual director were models of the priest/penitent relationship which the new rite of Penance is meant to establish.

In a period of economic recession, when a man's worth tends to be valued only by the size of his pay packet, Matt's attitude to work is illuminating. He was more than a conscientious worker, he was a considerate workmate. Though he could be happy spending long hours praying or reading, he found it hard to bear the enforced idleness of convalescence. He was determined not to be a burden on others, not even on the State, much less on his fellow workers. When families went hungry during the General Strike, Matt, a single man, gave his strike pay to men with wives and children dependent on them.

Today, when human rights are questioned, when the right to life itself is held cheap, Matt Talbot's staunch identification with his deprived fellow-members in the Union branch to which he belonged is an example. Last year the largest Trade Union in Ireland placed on record its pride in and appreciation of Matt, a "founder-member". The part he played was never divisive; he respected his employers. His charity reached across social barriers and class divisions.

In our endeavours to increase devotion to the Blessed Eucharist Matt Talbot's daily fidelity to Mass and Holy Communion is an inspiration. His faith in the Real Presence of Jesus in the Eucharist was expressed in his reverent deportment; his kneeling, bowed figure, his slow genuflections, his recollection and devotion showed how firmly he believed that the Eucharist is the Body of the Son of God made man.

We are witnessing in the Church today a great movement towards personal prayer. In this, too, our poor man of Dublin can teach us. When missing from his hospital ward he was found in the chapel. At slack periods in Martin's yard he hid himself between the stacks of timber—to pray. And, strangely, these hard-drinking, rough speaking men who worked with him did not resent this man whose style of life was so different to theirs. He reminds one of the Desert Fathers of old, seeking God in solitude and, having found him, being impelled to seek for and find God in others. There must be many Dublin dockers in heaven today because of the example given them by one of their own.

Miss Purcell quotes one of the foremen in T. & C. Martin's describing Matt:

> He never spoke about his good deeds. He was strict with himself, but quiet, kind and gentle with others. Everybody was fond of him; he had no enemies, all respected him. He never played up to people but spoke his mind frankly. He was not hot-headed, but solid and sensible. He was a diligent workman who did his work faithfully and did not waste his time. I never could find fault with his work and I never knew him to disobey an order. He did good turns for others whenever he could. He had an extraordinary influence over and power of handling men who were inclined to be bullies.

That sounds like a good character for a Christian. Is it too much to think that it is also a charter for sanctity? Matt Talbot's life was truly that of a prophet. May he and his message be received in his own country—and everywhere.

✠ Dermot

19 November, 1976.

Archbishop of Dublin

CHAPTER I

IN THE EARLY AUTUMN OF 1853 A MARRIAGE took place at Clontarf, a seaside village two miles to the north-east of Dublin. The priest who performed the ceremony entered the usual particulars in the parish register: the contracting parties, Charles Talbot and Elizabeth Bagnall; the witnesses, Thomas Mills and Anne Kelly; his own signature, Edward Kennedy, C.C.; and the date, September 19th, 1853.

It was probably a very ordinary wedding—except for the two most concerned. The marriage of a dock labourer and his girl would not attract much notice, even though bride and groom wore the best they could buy or borrow for the occasion. In any case, the Clontarf villagers of a century ago would have had little time to stand and stare in September—their busiest season. The sea-water was at its best then and bathers had to be fetched into and out of Dublin Bay—for a consideration. Besides, the oysters were in, and during September, the first of the months "with an R," work on the oyster-beds was in full swing. In Clontarf, that village described by a writer of the gay 'nineties as "drowsy, behind the times, rendered insupportable by the smell of rotting seaweed and the sight of its disreputable bathing machines ...." not many would have had time, even had they the inclination, to be onlookers at the humble Talbot-Bagnall wedding.

Charles Talbot was then thirty. Speaking of him a century later, one who knew him in his forties described him as having been of uncommonly small stature, and—as is not unusual in men cast in the mould of Zaccheus—of rather aggressive bearing. His bride Elizabeth, then not quite twenty, was plain-looking. Of her life previous to her marriage nothing is known. Her

9

name does not appear in the Clontarf Baptismal registers, which go back a few decades from 1853, nor in other north city parish registers of the time. It is possible that she worked in that parish and was married from her employer's house. Then as now marriages usually took place in the parish where the bride had lived before her wedding-day.

In 1853 Charles Talbot was in fairly regular employment. He was one of a class of workers known as Preferable Labourers, labourers who enjoyed rights of precedence when the firm with which they were "listed" took on extra men. The Corporation for Preserving and Improving the Port of Dublin(a body later superseded by the Dublin Port and Docks Board) had among its permanent employees Robert Talbot, the father of Charles. Permanent employees could get their immediate relatives on to the Preferable Labourers' List of the firm by which they themselves were employed, so Charles Talbot owed his place on the Port Authority list to the fact that his father was a permanent employee of that concern. The Port of Dublin was a busy one; shipping doubled between 1836 and 1856 and more than trebled between 1836 and 1866; hence, the newly-married Charles Talbot, though not in permanent employment, would have been seldom unemployed.

The Talbots first set up house in a room in Lower Rutland Street. It was a street similar to many in the north-central sector of the city at that time. A few residents still clung desperately to the gentility that had been theirs in the days when the high and mighty lived in mansions a few doors up or down the street. The names of the householders in 1853 included Rintoul, Pasley, Hales,

Acheson, Stubbs, Eykelbosch, Babington, d'Aubertin and Crabbe—surnames which lent the neighbourhood a slightly distinguished, if alien, air. In No. 26 a Miss Connors taught Female Infants. From No. 7 to No. 16, and from No. 35 to No. 46, placards read "Building Ground"; indeed, the same melancholy announcement was repeated at various intervals all along Rutland Street, Upper and Lower. For over fifty years fashionable Dublin had been following the lead given by the Earl of Kildare in moving from the north to the south of the Liffey, and by the middle of the nineteenth century Rutland Street was but one of the former residential· areas where sites were selling cheaply; in that hitherto select street the Post Office Directory for 1853 listed seven houses as tenements.

At the time of his marriage Charles Talbot was earning about 15s. a week. Wages at any given place or period cannot be considered apart from the cost of living. In 1853 eggs were a penny apiece, farmers' butter one and three a pound; beef was fivepence a pound, mutton sixpence halfpenny; a pig's cheek cost ninepence, a large loaf threepence; best Clontarf oysters were one and six a dozen in season, ale was twopence a glass, and Imperial porter—with emphasis on *Imperial*—tuppence a pint. Top coats, Melton cloth for gentlemen, Uncle Tom and Topsy styles for ladies, were selling for twenty shillings in the Sackville Street shops. Tailored trousers cost a guinea, and copies of the elegant straw bonnets the Queen had worn on her visit to Ireland could be had for half a crown.

A review published in the *Dublin Journal of Medical Science* in May, 1845, regarding the housing conditions obtaining in the Dublin of the time, particularly in the

11

"Liberties," gave this description of the dwellings in St Michan's parish:

> A large proportion of the houses have not necessaries and those that have are in a very few instances connected with a sewer, but must be emptied by carrying out through the house. Water closets are scarcely known unless in public buildings; there may not be above a dozen in the entire district .... Of those houses let to weekly tenants not one in ten has the water conveyed into it by branch from the street main. The tenants in such cases are dependent for their supply on the public fountain .... The water is not constantly on in these fountains. The wretched people have no vessels to contain a supply; the kettle and the broken jar are the only ones to be seen in these abodes of misery. Nothing marks their poverty more than when congregating round the public fountain, struggling to have their little supply. There are many lanes and courts in which a tumbler of water could not be had fit for drinking ....
> ... In some rooms in these situations it is not an unfrequent occurrence to see above a dozen human beings crowded into a space not fifteen feet square. Within this space the food of these beings, such as it is, must be prepared; within this space they must eat and drink; men, women and children must strip, dress and sleep."

A French priest-writer, l'Abbé Perraud, in his *Etudes sur l'Irlande Contemporaine,* published in 1862, gave a grim picture of the dwellings of the Dublin poor. He found in the Liberties, he said, wretched rooms into which were packed poor families—victims of the agricultural revolution that had torn them so violently from their labours in the fields. Houses to the number of 8,000, about one-third of the total houses in the city, were let in rooms to the poor and the lowest-paid labourers. Of Dublin's population of 250,000 some 64,000 occupied these houses which were mostly in dark alleys and damp courts. Five, six and seven persons lived where only two or three could live with ease. Perraud computed that the average weekly wage in Dublin then was 8s. 6d. for men, 4s. 11d. for women, and 3s. 9d. for those under age. This evidence of dire poverty and bad housing conditions explains the appalling death-roll when cholera epidemics broke out in 1832, 1867, and at other times during the century. In his *History of Medicine in Ireland* Dr John Fleetwood states that 5,600 died of cholera in Dublin in one year alone; he also states that the maternal mortality rate for the city was 20% for the first half of the century.

Many survivors of the famines of the 'forties had begged their way to Dublin. In 1861, when Matt Talbot was five years of age, Dr Cullen, Dublin's Archbishop, appeared as a witness before the Poor Law Commission. After giving harrowing evidence regarding conditions in the South Dublin Union, where four thousand wretched creatures were herded together anyhow, His Grace said:

> What is the actual state of affairs in that institution? Poor infants are brought to an untimely end ... Corruption and profligacy have been promoted by the mixture of degradation and innocence. Family ties are broken. The old and infirm pine away in misery and suffering, in bitterness and affliction. Religion and charity have been banished. Povery is not relieved but the poor are destroyed and demoralised .... And I would like to put any gentleman here upon the diet given there—two meals a day, a little oatmeal and milk in the morning; soup and bread for dinner, and that every day in the year, except Easter Sunday and Christmas Day, on which days ladies and gentlemen go to the workhouses to enjoy the sight, just as they might go to see wild beasts feeding.

As was to be expected, many poor persons preferred to roam the streets, to beg and steal, sooner than go to the workhouses. The city literally swarmed with beggars, some professional mendicants, others who had been used to better days but whom the Great Hunger or the Crowbar Brigades had reduced to penury. As always, the poor were the best friends of the poor; in the poorer areas of Dublin, such as the Rutland Street-North Strand area where the Talbots lived, the residents, though mostly in very humble circumstances themselves, managed to spare a little for the utterly destitute.

Little did Elizabeth Talbot think, when she settled down in No. 2 Rutland Street in 1853 that within the next twenty years, she would change her address no less than eleven times. From the time of her marriage to her death sixty years later she was to know eighteen different homes. Could she see those ˜eighteen "flittings"—one almost every second year for the first twenty years of her married life—her heart might well have failed her on that September day in 1853.

There were plenty of entertainments at which the newly-weds might have celebrated their weekend honeymoon. Signora Pauline Violante, Rope Dancer and Ascensionist, was drawing crowds to the Portobello Gardens. A heart-rending play, *Rent Day,* was on at the Royal, while the Rotunda Gardens displayed

The Wonders of the Human Creation
THE AZTEC LILLIPUTIANS
A new race of people hitherto
supposed to be fabulous or extinct
Unique, Strange Beautiful Creatures
Music: *The Aztec Polka.* 1s. Admission

Perhaps the greatest attraction, free of charge, was the sale of the property and effects of Kirwan, arraigned a few months previously for the Howth murder. The auction lasted several days and there was spirited bidding for the chattels of the most talked-of man of his city and decade. The thrill of going out to Ireland's Eye, to look at the rock where the body was found, had worn away. There was no rock left, as English visitors, glad of some grim souvenir of a summer sojourn in Ireland, had removed splinter by splinter and scrap by scrap the jagged spar that had been the last resting-place of the unfortunate Mrs Kirwan.

The Talbots could have gone to the Phoenix Park, where Franconi's Imperial Circus—with real Sikhs—was staging the Battle of Gujrat. To make things more realistic, the Battle was timed to coincide with the Field Day of Her Majesty's Forces drawn from the various Dublin military barracks. But Elizabeth's friends would have warned her that the Park was no place to bring a husband; before you knew where you were the recruiting sergeants would inveigle him into "taking the shilling." With the Russians massing in Sebastopol, wherever that was, and the hateful Louis Napoleon, whoever he was, plotting and planning, new husbands were best kept away from the Field Day in the Park.

There were other sights to see. The Lady Aeronaut, Mrs Graham, went up in a balloon of Indian cane at one side of the Liffey-mouth and landed safely at Clontarf. A magnetic-telegraph line was being laid in the city's main thoroughfare, Sackville Street. Nearby on Carlisle Bridge there was a colourful display of dahlias. The great Industrial Exhibition in Merrion Square was still open; even Queen Victoria had been amazed at the wonders shown there when she visited it a month previously. At the

15

entrance-wickets visitors were warned to beware of thieves. The notorious Bill Coffey and his Swell Mob had, true to their title, visited the Exhibition in style, going away richer than they arrived, having stolen a diamond brooch and other valuables. Six clay pipes vanished also, but Coffey and his accomplices were not blamed for that plebeian theft.

The house, No. 2, Rutland Street, in which the Talbots lived after their marriage, cannot have been too dilapidated for, in the Directories of a few years later, the same address is listed as a Select School for the Daughters of Gentlefolk. When Charles and Elizabeth Talbot set up their first home together in their native city, Dublin had a population of a quarter of a million. The city proper covered an area of about 3,500 acres in extent and was almost enclosed in the nine-mile-circuit formed by North and South Circular Roads. The Kingstown and Dalkey Railway connected Bray and intervening villages with the city.

The first four children born to the Talbots were baptised in the principal church of Dublin Archdiocese, the Pro-Cathedral. John Joseph, the eldest, was born in 1854; by 1855 the parents had changed from Rutland Street to 13 Aldborough Court* and were living close to one of the biggest and busiest military barracks in Ireland: in that year Aldborough seethed with activity, for the Crimean War was on.

Charles Talbot's wife missed the celebrations on the first Friday of May 1856. She was not among the crowds lining the route of the Peace Proclamation procession. She

---

*Only a trace of Aldborough Court now remains, the area having been practically demolished when a bomb was dropped there accidentally by a German plane in 1941.

did not see the Lord Lieutenant, resplendent in scarlet and silver, ride by on his favourite bay. She did not hear him proclaim the peace concluded between Her Majesty the Queen and His Imperial Highness, the Tsar of all the Russias, nor the full-throated roar of applause that followed. She was absent that evening when her neighbours in Aldborough Court, off Dublin's North Strand Road, turned out to watch the fireworks display and to cheer the Cheshire Militia on their way back to Aldborough Barracks. Elizabeth Talbot had more pressing, more personal concerns just then. On that day, 2 May 1856, her second son, the child she would call Matthew, was born.

The Crimean War, 'a small, unsuccessful, horribly mismanaged war' was over. The survivors had not yet returned. Some would never see Dublin again. Their bones lay whitening on the heights of Balaclava, for they had had the misfortune to be under the command of those rival incompetents, Lord Lucan and Lord Cardigan, jointly responsible for the disastrous charge of the Light Brigade. It was the decade after the famines, the decade before the Fenians. Patriotism was at a low ebb, national spirit moribund, pride of race seemingly extinct.

Dubliners who strolled along the quays that May evening, admiring the Liffey bridges decorated for the celebrations, had forgotten that their fathers saw those same bridges festooned with corpses of men executed after the '98 rebellion. On the following Monday morning Her Majesty's inspectors would require Irish children to declaim 'with suitable expression', verses from the school texts approved for use in Ireland, verses such as—

I thank the goodness and the grace
That on my birth have smiled,
And made me in these Christian days
A happy English child.

Into that Ireland, to all appearances subjugated, Matt Talbot was born.

He was baptised in the Pro-Cathedral by Father James Mulligan, a young priest only five years ordained. There is an error in the entry made that day in the baptismal register, Elizabeth Talbot's maiden name having been given as Mullock instead of Bagnall. Sir Joseph Glynn, in his *Life of Matt Talbot*,gives an explanation of this error:

> The parochial clergy state that a very common error is for the woman who carries the infant to the church to give her own name when questioned, instead of the name of the mother. In the present instance this must have occurred, as Mullock is the name of cousins of the Talbots, and nothing is more probable than that a cousin carried the child to the church.

Shortly after Matthew's birth the Talbots left Aldborough Court for No. 16, Summerhill, where Robert was born in 1858. Then they moved to No. 3, Summerhill, where the first girl, Maria, was born in 1860. In 1862, when the twins, Edward and Charles, were born, the family moved again, this time to Newcomen Court, off the North Strand. They were now in St Agatha's Parish, so the twins were the first of the family to be baptised in St Agatha's, North William Street. Charles was called after his father but he must have died in infancy as, later on, another baby was christened Charles; the other twin, Edward, may be also presumed to have died at an early age as a nonagenarian who died in 1953 and who remembered and could supply details about the other Talbot boys never heard of an Edward.

The seventh of Charles and Elizabeth's rapidly increasing flock, Philip, was born in 1864, in Newcomen Court; he grew up to be the wild boy of the family and was nick-named "the Man" Talbot. The Talbots "flitted" further afield sometime between 1864 and 1867; one boy, Joseph, whose baptismal entry has not been traced, is remembered by several old men as coming next in age to Philip. While Philip was still an infant his parents—by this time probably having a bit of trouble finding accommodation for themselves and their care—moved back again to the Pro-Cathedral parish. Early in 1867 Elizabeth was born at 47 Montgomery Street; a few months later the family was again living at Newcomen Court, but, by 1868, there was another "flitting," this time to Byrne's Lane, a long since demolished huddle of six cottages off Potters' Alley, between Lower Abbey Street and Marlborough Lane. The following year found them back again in Summerhill, this time at No. 10 where Patrick was born. The year 1871 saw poor Mrs Talbot making another move, when they returned to St Agatha's parish, to Love Lane, Ballybough; Susan was born at Love Lane and there, too, in 1874 was born the last of Charles and Elizabeth Talbot's twelve children.

When this last baby, the second to be called Charles, was born, the older boys were working. John was twenty, Matt eighteen, Bob sixteen and Mary fourteen. In those days children went to work at twelve and even younger. The Talbot boys got work as helpers, runners and messengers here and there. Once turned sixteen, however, thanks to their father and grandfather, they were taken on by the Port and Docks Board, at boys' wages of six shillings a week—with prospects.

During these twenty-one years, Charles Talbot's wages

rose a little. Instead of the fifteen shillings he earned when he was married he now got eighteen shillings a week, being in charge of one of the whiskey stores at the Custom House Docks. By modern standards his wages and his sons' wages seem hopelessly inadequate, but by comparison with those of other *skilled* workers of the time, the Port and Docks rates and hours were reasonably good. The silk weavers, dependent on a doomed industry, frequently found that their pay had dropped to 8s. and even as low as 4s. weekly, when the machines began to take over from the hand-looms. Canal-boat men got 10s. a week, and a captain 12s.; bricklayers and carpenters averaged 16s. to 18s. a week, painters 18s. to £1 a week. Ship-carpenters and printers ranged from £1 to 24s.

The wages of the Talbot boys were well over the average of 3s. 9d. weekly and their hours were good in comparison with those of youths in the bakery and similar trades who worked from 5 a.m. to 9 p.m. *seven* days a week. Besides, the Talbots probably considered themselves lucky to be employed at all, as it was a time of industrial decline. In a study by Charles Booth in Coyne's *Ireland, Industrial and Agricultural,* some vital statistics are given. Before the famine, Ireland had 969,000 workers to England's 604,000 in the textile and dyeing industries. By 1881 Ireland had only 130,000 to England's 962,000 in the same trades. In the same period, building and manufacturing trades lost 626,000 workers, but general labourers increased from 31,000 to 144,000, and shirt-making, "the last refuge of destitute women," employed nearly double as many as formerly; domestic servants were also a class greatly increased in number—one had to eat to live and a position that promised regular meals was most popular in a land still in the shadow of the Great Hunger.

A little attention to the Directories of the period 1853 to 1874, enables us to follow the odyssey of the Tablots more closely. The first home, though listed as "tenements," had a Poor Law Valuation of £16, and the fact that a Miss Shanley set up her Select Seminary for the Daughters of Gentlefolk at that address a few years later, indicates that it must have been in fairly good repair. The Aldborough Court houses, just off the North Strand, were listed as "thirty-seven small houses; P.L.V. £1 10s. to £10." Here Matthew was born in No. 13. A very few years later the Directories listed all the Aldborough Court houses as tenements, with the exception of No. 18, the residence of one James Larkin, carrier. No. 16, Summerhill, was in the midst of tenements, the P.L.V. of which was £3 to £17. No. 3, Summerhill, to which they moved in 1860, was over a shop—"Hughes; Provision Dealer; P.L.V. £13." It is interesting to note that the occupiers of the Summerhill houses bore surnames more Irish in origin than the Talbot's former genteel neighbours in Rutland Street; besides Mr Hughes, there were Walshes, Murrays, Ryans, Powells and Pollards.*

After the birth of the twins in 1862, the family moved to Newcomen Court, which consisted of "nineteen tenements; P.L.V. £3 to £6." These must have been very wretched houses, for after 1865 the Directories did not consider them worth listing; yet, the Talbots were back there in the May of 1867, that being the address given

* When James Stephens escaped from Richmond jail on November 25th, 1865, he was hidden in the house of a poor woman, Mrs Butler, of Summerhill. Although the Castle offered £1,000 for his apprehension, and though several people in Summerhill area must have known of the Fenian leader's hiding-place, the £1,000 went unclaimed, and a few months later Stephens sailed for France.

when John and Matthew were first entered on the rolls of O'Connell School. The move to Montgomery Street was definitely a move-up, probably warranted by John's having started work; in this locality business was brisk; there were few tenements in Montgomery Street; big timber and slate yards jostled one another, while saw-mills and corn and flour-mills raised a perpetual din; there were several vintners, some grocers' shops, dairies, a boot-and-shoe maker, a coach-maker, at least five "yards" and a lodging-house or two, the street's proximity to Amiens Street railway station, built in 1843, having, no doubt, helped trade.

By 1868 Matt, too, was working—at least by the end of that year. He was a messenger for Burkes of the North Lotts. In that same year for the first time the Talbots had a house of their own; not much of a house, but a house for all that—one of the cottages in Byrne's Lane. These are given in the Directories for that year as "six cottages; P.L.V. £1 5s." A few years later the Byrne's Lane dwellings were demolished. In 1869 the Talbots moved again to No. 10, Summerhill, a house they shared with a carpenter named Ryan. They spent nearly three years at this address, the longest period in any one place up to 1874. In 1871 they were at 5, Love Lane, Ballybough, in the worst tenements they had encountered in all their changes of address: "Seventeen tentements; P.L.V. £1 to £5 10s." is the Directory description of these houses, which were pulled down a few years later. They were now a family of at least eleven; it is certain that nine, if not more, of the children grew to adult age. While they were in Love Lane, three of the boys were working and possibly the oldest girl, and the father's wages had increased by one-fifth. Yet, the period from 1874 to 1884 saw them living in very poor circumstances, the reasons for which may be deduced later on. Sometime in the later 1870s they moved to Newcomen Avenue, off the North Strand, a street of thirty small cottages, one of which they occupied.

Elizabeth Talbot, by the time she was twenty-five years married, had borne twelve children—perhaps more—and had reared at least nine of these; she had known eleven different homes. An old man, Pat Doyle, who died in December, 1953, aged over ninety years, was, in his young days, a boon companion of Bob, Phil and Joe Talbot. He gave the following recollections of the family:

> Mrs Talbot was a very hard-working woman. She had to be, with such a houseful of them. Sometimes she used to go out charing. Indeed, she had her hands full with the lot of them. Especially with Phil, "the Man" Talbot, who was my own age or a little younger and who was terrible wild, even as a chap.

The clerk of St Agatha's Church, eighty-one-years-old Thomas Ward, who grew up in Newcomen Avenue, tells more about Phil Talbot:

> He used to come rolling up Summerhill of a Saturday, shouting "I'm the Man—Talbot." That was how he came to be called "The Man." He was a terror for the drink; they all were, but he was the worst, and very contrary when he had enough taken.

Both of these men remembered the father of the family, Charles Talbot, as a very small man "with a very loud voice for the size of him." He was inclined to be truculent and "hard to manage" when he had a drop taken. Pat Doyle declared (and the Port and Docks Board's records bear him out in this) that it was John Talbot, the eldest son, and not his father, Charles—as was commonly believed—who reached a responsible position with that concern. A few months before being pensioned off in 1887, Charles Talbot was made under-foreman at 21s. a week; on his retirement he got 6s. 8d. a week pension, which was increased to 10s. a week in 1884. He lived until 1889.

Pat Doyle also added these remarks:

> All the Talbots, father and sons, drank; all barring John, the eldest. He was the only steady fellow of them when they were young men. Himself—old Charlie—and the boys were always arguing; they were a famous lot for arguing—always at it. On Saturdays when they'd all have a good drop in—all except John—'tis they were the contrary lot. Mrs Talbot had a hard time of it, trying to keep the peace; but she could manage them all right. And John was a good, steady fellow. He was like his mother.

This was the family and these several addresses in the North Strand area the homes in which Matt Talbot, born in May, 1856, grew to boyhood and manhood.

(Note: The introduction of decimal currency in Ireland in February 1971 and the fluctuating value of sterling—with its recent rapid depreciation —means that figures for wages, prices etc., given in this book bear no relation to present figures. The Central Statistics Office states that the purchasing power of £1 in 1850 approximates to the purchasing power of £17.53 in 1976.)

CHAPTER II

ON MAY 6th, 1867, JOHN AND MATTHEW TALBOT were entered on the Rolls of the Christian Brothers' School at North Richmond Street—O'Connell School. This is the entry:

Date of Admission: May 6th, 1867.
No. on Registry: 1402.
Pupil's Name: John Talbot.
Residence: Newcomen Court.
Age: 12.
Class admitted into: Reading, 3; Arithmetic, 1;
  Grammar, 1; Geography, 1.
Occupation of Parents: Labourer.
General Observations: —

Date of Admission: May 6th, 1867.
No. on Registry: 1403.
Pupil's Name: Matthew Talbot.
Residence: Newcomen Court.
Age: 9.
Class admitted into: Reading, 2.
Occupation of Parents: Labourer.
General Observations: —

It will be noted that Matthew's age was entered incorrectly; he was then just eleven. In the Roll the original entry was obviously 11; the left-hand digit was afterwards crossed out and the right-hand one altered to 9. Several people who knew Matt Talbot in his later years stated that he was a very small man; in all probability he was undersized for his years when a boy. The morning he was enrolled he would have been interrogated concerning his age; it is quite conceivable that his teacher, Brother Ryan, having first entered eleven—the age given him by either Matt or John or Mrs Talbot—decided on second thoughts that the smaller of the Talbot boys could not be the eleven years he claimed to be.

Matt Talbot was put into a rather "special" class. At that time, when compulsory school attendance was unthought of and when many poor parents kept their children at home lest proselytising take place in the name of what then passed for "National" education, the Christian Brothers rallied to the help of the neglected boys in the neighbourhoods of their schools. They had special classes for lads whose education had been neglected and whose time for study would be necessarily short. Boys who availed themselves of these classes were taught to read and write; they learned their prayers, the essential truths and practices of their Faith, and they were prepared for Confession, Holy Communion and Confirmation.

The Christian Brothers' *Second Book*, as it was called, would have cost young Matt Talbot eightpence. It was Catholic in tone and covered a wide variety of subjects. The Sacred History lessons had been adapted from the Scriptures by no less a pen than Gerald Griffin's. Two-hundred-word biographies of St Patrick, St Vincent de Paul, St John of God and other saints were interspersed with lessons on science and nature study. There were homilies on hygiene, while period pieces with explanatory titles—The Thoughtless Boy, The Honest Sweep, How to be Satisfied, Generosity, Honesty Rewarded and Evil of Law—imparted the authentic Victorian tinge. As for History and Geography, Ireland, England and Scotland got two pages each, and some World Geography was taught indirectly by means of lessons on oranges, tea, sugar and similar commodities. The first lesson Matt Talbot encountered was entitled *In The Presence of God*.Having mastered the alphabet and the triple lists of nouns, verbs and adjectives standing sentinel above his lesson, he probably chanted with his class:

We can form no idea of the delights which God has in store for those who love Him. The eye has not seen it, nor the ear heard it, nor can the heart of man conceive it . . . .

We should never forget God. If a child would only accustom himself to say some prayers from time to time during the day, he would soon acquire the habit of thinking of God.

These prayers may be very short, such as, "O my God, I love you"; "My whole desire is to please you"; "I will do this for your honour and glory" . . . .

. . .If a child be faithful in this holy practice for some time, he will feel how delightful it is to enjoy God's presence . . . . The remembrance of God's presence will regulate his whole conduct.

Then there came a short but grim lesson on coal followed by a lesson on a garden, which latter was probably as much outside the Talbot boys' experience as a coal-mine. After these three lessons came—delightful variation!—the first poem Matt Talbot ever read. It was to Our Blessed Lady:

Mother of Mercy! day by day
My love of thee grows more and more:
Thy gifts are strewn upon my way,
Like sands upon the great sea-shore.

Though poverty and work and woe
The masters of my life, may be,
When times are worst, who does not know
Darkness is light with love of thee?

27

Always a favourite hymn with the old Dublin confraternities, it would have been well-known by the families of the boys attending O'Connell School. When, at noon each day in that May of 1867, the boys assembled for hymns and the Litany of Our Blessed Lady, the puny Matt Talbot probably made himself heard. The late Mr William Larkin and Mr Paddy Laird, who both remembered Matt in the Men's Sodality of the Immaculate Conception attached to St Francis Xavier's Church in Gardiner Street, said that he had a pleasant singing voice. "But a big voice," added Mr Larkin, "for his size; you wouldn't know where a man so small got such a powerful voice." Old Pat Doyle partly explained this: "Matt had a great shout, though he was such a bit of a man; but sure the father had the very same—you'd hear old Charlie a mile away if one of the lads 'ruz' his temper." Young Brother Ryan—himself a fine singer—who had charge of this class of late-to-come, soon-to-go pupils, who was so incredulous that he wrote nine years when Matthew Talbot shouted "eleven," must have looked with interest on the under-sized lad who sang with an outsize voice.

On January 24th, 1968—the following year—Matthew Talbot (then living in Byrne's Lane) was entered on the rolls of O'Connell School again. He and sixteen other boys were all enrolled on the same day. This time his age is given as ten, his father's occupation is given as "cooper," and he again takes up as a "Beginner at Book 2." He attended until May of that year and got some marks under "Proficiency" before he left. He could read the Second Book; in Arithmetic he had mastered "General Principles, Notation, Numeration, Addition, Subtraction and Simple Multiplication." He had done "General Outline of Grammar and Orthography," and had made the acquaintance of such Geogrphical ideas as oceans, continents, and "estimated populations." All of which—in addition to having been prepared to receive the Sacraments and getting a grounding in the truths and practice of religion—was no small achievement on the part of his teacher. Brother Ryan, no doubt, would have done far better but for one thing: Matthew Talbot was a bad attender. In the Brother's hand-writing is registered opposite the name Matthew Talbot—for all the world to read—the laconic comment "A Mitcher."

The enrolment of seventeen boys from the poorer areas round O'Connell's in the second week after school re-opened that January, is not without interest. Less than a month previously, Cardinal Cullen, spearhead of the counter-attack against the proselytisers, asked his priests for still greater efforts, still more ceaseless vigilance in protecting their flocks against what most Irish Catholics regarded as something worse than all the confiscations, all the plantations, all the injustices, oppression, misrule and cruelty of preceding centuries.

Legislation compelling school attendance was still in the future, but to understand fully why children like the Talbots were not attending any school until John was in his thirteenth year and Matthew just over eleven, it is necessary to recall some of the happenings in Dublin in the 1850s and 1860s.

Soon after the end of the Crimean War, Dublin, like other cities where the British Army had strong garrisons, began to suffer from the inevitable backwash of the conflict. Maimed soldiers and disbanded militia-men crowded every troopship that steamed into Dublin Bay. In the wake of these warriors came the rag-tag-and-bobtail who, having trailed various armies for the duration of the campaign, made sure to return with the victors. The English authorities, finding London swamped by these undesirables, drained the overflow to Ireland, and soon, into the backlanes and alleys of Dublin, the rejects of Europe swarmed.

The new arrivals were of several nationalities, yet they were people of no nation, unloyal rather than disloyal, caring neither for England nor Ireland, nor even for the land that gave them birth. They were faithful to no leader, devoted to no cause, acknowledged no authority. The men were lawless, cunning—the stuff of which mobs are made—the women utterly depraved. Being penniless, most of these immigrants drifted to the poorer areas of Ireland's capital. The streets near a big military barracks attracted greater numbers of such foreigners than similar areas throughout the city; many would have tried to fit themselves in, somehow, to the already overcrowded North Strand district, to be near Aldborough Barracks, at which was quartered the Commissariat Staff Corps, that being the central depot for supplies for the 137,000 troops considered necessary to maintain English law and order in Ireland.

The following testimony was given at the first Enquiry on Matt Talbot by Mr William J. Larkin, since deceased.*

> The area in which Matt's home was situated (North Strand area) was, at the time of his childhood and youth, very disorderly. There were in the district many brothels,

---

* A Diocesan Tribunal known as the Ordinary or Informative Process conducted the earlier Enquiry into the life and virtues of Matt Talbot. Its sessions began in 1931 and continued until 1937. The more recent Tribunal which sat from 1948 to 1952 was the Apostolic Process.

which were much frequented by members of the British Army. Publilc houses, were liquor was sold, were very numerous in the area whether licensed or unlicensed, and consequently there were many temptations in the way of a young man. Matt fell into the vice of drunkenness, but I never heard it said that he indulged in impurity.

The post-Crimean influx was bad. But worse was to come. Wave after wave of zealots descended upon Ireland. Society after society was established to spread alleged light in a land supposedly sunk in darkness and error. Titled persons—some but a few generations removed from the mercenary soldier or shrewd sutler who had grabbed opportunity, wealth and lands at the right moment and quickly vaulted from the common estate to ready-made nobility—lent their names, influence, time and money to schemes for weaning the Irish from the "Papist superstitions" to which they so tenaciously clung. Handbills were thrust in at doorways; children playing in the lanes were bribed into taking pamphlets home; posters offensive and often blasphemous, advertised insults from every hoarding. On the street-corners there were paid preachers, mostly ignorant men, glad to earn good money for denying and deriding the most sacred Catholic beliefs and devotions. In the Post Office Directory for the 1850s and 1860s some of the Societies are listed. There were Societies for Reforming, Educating, Improving, Suppressing, Relieving, Bettering, Supporting and Evangelising the citizens of Dublin and the people of Ireland.

To the Dublin citizens—the first to meet each succeeding wave of invaders, colonisers and adventurers from "over the water," the populace coerced and intimidated for so long by Crown troops and by Castle police—these hordes of proselytisers must have seemed the last straw. A re-incarnated Cromwell could hardly have been more unedurable. But the very poor, on whom the brunt of this attack fell, rose nobly to the occasion. One has only to recall the Dublin ballad singers' retaliatory efforts against the Soupers' Hymns and Songs of Truth to appreciate the metal of which the Dublin character is forged. Matt Talbot and his brothers and sisters could have heard street-singers drawing the crowds in the North Strand area with the Ballad of the Bird's Nest: *

Her child she sold for paltry gold,
To Kingstown he did go, ma'am,
From the mother's breast to the vulture's nest:
The robin will soon be a crow, ma'am.

And Mrs Talbot, like all her neighbours, would have heard the satire on a certain infamous Mrs MacGrane who had gone up in the world but down in her fellow-Catholics' estimation:

Arrah, Mrs MacGrath, did you hear the news?
But, of course, my jewel, you knew it;
The Quality's goin' to save our souls
An' pay us for letting them do it.
There's Mrs MacGrane, when her man was slain
On the banks of the bowld Crimea,
Gave her clergy up for the bit an' the sup,
An' took to Luther's idea.

---

* Some orphanages, noted for the proselytising activities they carried on under the guise of charity and zeal for poor children, were nick-named "Birds' Nests."

The old Irish air, *Nora Chriodhna,* then getting a new lease of life as a popular Lancers tune at Castle Balls, was given a different popularity up and down the city's main thoroughfare, when the successors of the greatly missed ballad-singer and rhymster, Zosimus, exhorted citizens thus:

> *O, come with me to Merrion Square,*
> *An', sure as me name is Reilly,*
> *Each murdherin' thief will get mutton an' beef*
> *If he prays with Mrs Smyly.*

The young Talbots were probably among the groups of children who, with more zeal than manners, were found—at a safe distance—encircling a disseminator of handbills or a street-evangelist, singing in shrill voices:

> *Souper, Souper, ring yer bell,*
> *Souper, Souper, go to hell!*

Their mothers would have warned them again and again of what could happen to children who listened to such people. If they were not more careful they might end up locked inside one of Mrs Smyly's Homes; then their tune would be changed to:

> *I smile and smile and smile,*
> *For I'm a Smyly boy,*
> *And buns and cake and jam*
> *Fill me with holy joy.*

Only a decade before, one hundred and twenty children of Catholic parentage were found to be in the hands of a Society, operating in Greystones area. Margaret Aylward, later to become Foundress of the Sisters of the Holy Faith, was ceaseless in her efforts to protect the children of the poor from being robbed of their religion. In 1857 she was responsible for saving forty children in danger of being handed over *en masse*. In 1860 Miss Aylward, then fifty, served six months in Grangegorman Female Penitentiary for having refused to surrender four-year-old Mary Matthews, whose dying father, a Catholic, wished her to be brought up in his own faith. By 1864 Dublin had become used to seeing Miss Aylward's Ladies, in their "black dresses and collars, chenille head nets, black lace veils and black cashmere capes with buttons," on their way to their first four Ragged Schools. Wherever the proselytisers were busy, there one would find either one of Margaret Aylward's or the Christian Brothers' schools springing up, almost overnight in some cases, to better the offer of free but often anti-Catholic education. They met the challenge of the proselytisers with the Catholic School, long denied the children of Irish Catholics.

But behind Miss Aylward, behind the Christian Brothers, stood the unyielding, granite-like, rather solitary figure of Cardinal Cullen, upon whose shoulders God had laid the care of a great Archdiocese. Like many strong characters, Paul Cullen escaped neither the calumny of his enemies nor the misunderstanding of his own people. The London *Times* called him "the great embroiderer of damaged escutcheons—the athletic Catholic whitewasher . . . a cold bigot . . . noted for his steady and unflinching opposition to the policy of England." The Dublin *Evening Mail*, censuring the choice of Dr Cullen as Dr Murray's successor, declared him to be "the person most obnoxious to the English government." On another occasion the same paper alluded to him as "the son of a half-hanged traitor," the reference being to the fact that his father narrowly escaped execution in the post '98 days. His opposition to the Fenian movement drew upon him the contumely of such men as Lucas, Gavin Duffy, Davitt and the Keatings.*

Yet, as an administrator, as a reformer, as a standard-raiser in secular and clerical education, he was for Ireland what Olier and Vincent de Paul had been for France.

In his forty-eighth year Dr Cullen was consecrated Archbishop of Armagh. Before that he had spent twenty-eight years in Rome as student and Professor and later as Rector of the Irish College. His work brought him into touch with Catholics from every country on earth and made him familiar with the problems confronting the Church everywhere. He was far-seeing and prudent, courageous and learned. After two years in Armagh he was called to the Archdiocese of Dublin where he had not one but several problems and difficulties.

He saw that the souper campaign, though wreaking great devastation, was a thing of mushroom growth; as with all fungi the period of its flourishing would be short-lived. But characteristically Dr Cullen set himself to examine why it had done such harm; he found it was

*Although the Cardinal was accused by the Fenians and their friends of being a frequent visitor to Dublin Castle in quest of favours for himself and his friends, the only time he *did* go there unasked, to seek a favour, was to save the life of a Fenian. Towards the end of 1867 General T. F. Burke (who had fought in the American Civil War) was sentenced to be hanged for his part in the '67 Rising—he was Commander in Tipperary. The scaffold had been erected when, on the very eve of the execution, Cardinal Cullen asked for and obtained a reprieve from the Castle authorities.

because the poor whom it sought to seduce were ill-taught, ignorant of their religion. "Thousands of the children of Dublin in their teens," wrote the late Canon E. J. Quigley in the *Irish Ecclesiastical Record*, "knew not the very essentials of the Catholic faith; the making of the Sign of the Cross was the height of knowledge and practice, and even prayer formulas taught by Christ and His Church, the *Pater* and *Ave*, were unknown to thousands of adults who claimed adherence to the one true fold." The Cardinal saw how the National System of Education was being gradually twisted into an instrument of proselytism. He gathered evidence; he studied the National System to see where its charter afforded him a loophole to demand fair play; having found Stanley's phrase "the National System must be one from which should be banished even the suspicion of proselytism," Dr Cullen took his stand upon it; he asked for no more; within that framework he saw that the System could become a means of great good.

Ireland's debt to Cardinal Cullen has been incalculable. For twenty-two years he supplied the driving force behind the forward progress of Catholicism; his people and priests had been for so long down-trodden that continuous direction, urging and ordering were necessary before the fetters struck loose by Catholic Emancipation in 1829 could be shaken off. Dr Cullen is remembered not for his achievements, the greatness of which neither his own nor succeeding generations have recognised, but for the two things that made him unpopular; patriots have seen nothing in him but a determined opponent of the Fenians; others tend to blame him for the disagreement and strained relations that arose between himself and the equally high-principled Dr Newman.

The Cardinal seems to have been a single-minded man. Coming to the capital at a time when the faith was being attacked and undermined in no uncertain fashion, he concentrated his energies on defending his flock from the menace of proselytism. But for his courage, foresight and sustained efforts, the Catholics of Dublin—and Ireland—might well have lost their schools and their faith. He had to reform. A generation only a few decades removed from the era of religious persecution stood in dire spiritual need.

Paul Cullen led them, despite their protests when the going became hard, force-marched them to safer terrain. He had to heal and then to make hardy; to be all-in-all to his flock and yet to urge them to unaided effort; he had to administer remedies and tonics not always palatable; to protect the menaced the while he himself faced and fought the attackers. In a word, he was a great reformer—a man in the tradition of St Charles Borromeo. Reformers, however, are seldom popular. Later generations may do justice to the memory of the prelate who made it possible for poor Catholics to get a Catholic education in the Dublin of his day. But for Cardinal Cullen, Matt Talbot would hardly have got the few lessons he did get:

In a Pastoral issued in June, 1856, Dr Cullen wrote:

> Posterity will with difficulty believe the great things achieved in the first half of the nineteenth century in favour of religion and education by the people of Ireland scarcely emerging from persecution; and this difficulty of belief will be increased by the consideration that millions were extorted at the same period from the poverty of the country for the support of an enormous Church Establishment, many of whose ministers are engaged in

assailing and maligning the doctrines and character of the people . . .

. . . Education, charity, the Bible, are now inscribed upon the banners of those who in past days delighted in persecution and in blood . . .

. . . Under these false colours, assumed for the purpose of deception, a system of pecuniary proselytism, having for its object to make converts by bribes and gold, has been established by the many bigoted and fanatical haters of Catholicity who abound . . . and an active and insidious war is carried on against our ancient and venerable Church . . .

He goes on to list twenty-one of the many Proselytising Societies. In that famous Pastoral of June 1856—for the Irish Bishops then issued several Pastorals each year—the Cardinal went on to refer to the huge sums of money being spent in attempts to pervert the Irish:

Many agents of the proselytising Societies are poor, ignorant men who undertake to insult and decry our religion for ten or fifteen shillings a week.

After summing up the methods used by the proselytisers—placards on the walls of the city, hand bills pushed under doors, published reports of anti-Catholic sermons and platform speeches—Dr Cullen continued:

. . . Many preachers devote themselves entirely to abusing Catholicism . . .(reference is then made to the bribes and gifts offered to obtain the perversion of the poor and destitute) . . . advantage being taken of the poverty caused by the famines of the previous decade and of the evictions that have filled Dublin with misery and want, thousands of victims of want or oppression crowding our streets . . . bigotry and fanaticism having determined to traffic on their misery.

Among the districts mentioned in the 1856 Pastoral of Dublin's Archbishop were Lurgan Street, the Coombe, Townsend Street and Rutland Street; these were listed as being the favourite hunting-grounds of the proselytisers. The Talbot family, though constantly changing residence, was seldom more than a few minutes' walk from Rutland Street where there was a school which dispensed not only education but various inducements calculated to win over to Protestantism the youngest and poorest Catholics in the neighbourhood.

Twice in the Spring of 1867, Dr Cullen in his Pastorals indicted the National System of Education, "which, though intended as a great boon and the means of uniting all classes, was turned to the purposes of proselytism."

Soon after a Pastoral dated April 30th, 1867 was read from every Catholic pulpit in Dublin, John and Matthew Talbot were sent to O'Connell School, to join a class for boys who had seldom gone to school and who could only spend a short time there. More significant is the re-enrolling of Matt and sixteen other boys in the January of 1868. A few weeks before that date, in the Discourse on Catholic Education given by the Cardinal to all the secular and regular clergy of the diocese, His Eminence denounced the school books in use in the schools under the National Board as containing nothing Catholic and "calculated to inspire a mere rationalistic spirit." He commended the schools of the Christian Brothers:

> ... where a good system of education prevails, the work
> commenced by parents is continued in the school, and
> children are taught, not merely the rudiments of secular

knowledge, but also the duties which as Catholics they are obliged to perform . . . The Christian Brothers teach their pupils to be good Christians and sincere Catholics. Children trained in this way will be useful members of society, and at the same time will be able to secure the end of their creation—the salvation of their souls. Yet the Commissioners of Education have adopted a rule by which Christian Brothers, and all men bound by vows, are excluded from teaching in the National Schools.

The Dublin Catholic of today reading that Discourse in very different times, finds its calm catalogue of injustice more moving than any impassioned appeal. How it must have stirred its hearers as that dreary year, '67—its weeks weighted with failure and disaster—drew to a close! Is it coincidence that there was a rounding-up of poor lads early in the New Year for that class regarded of so much importance by the Brothers that Room No. 1 was reserved for it?

Matt Talbot's teacher in O'Connell School, Brother Otteran Ryan, was then a young Brother in his 'teens. This is a description of him by a contemporary in records kept by the Christian Brothers:

I remember him, a youth of seventeen, of beautifully chiselled features, graceful and alert in form and movement, a soul befitting this environment, but further influenced by the fire of religious zeal chastened, however, by a most sweet temper. I can see him as he moved gracefully, still energetically, amongst his one hundred and twenty small but precious charges . . .

All through life he manifested the same affability and the same obliging disposition which, I must say, was often unreasonably called upon, for whoever wanted a favour, especially in the line of Art, was sure to write to Brother Otteran who knew not how to decline a request from a Brother in need of help.

The Obituary Notice goes on to tell that the Brother excelled in illuminative art, becoming expert as a copyist of 13th century illuminated work. He was also highly accomplished musician and choir-master. The late Dr Vincent O'Brien, one of the best-loved men in the Dublin of his time—the renowned musician and teacher to whom the world owes, among others, John McCormack—was a pupil of Brother Ryan's. The good Brother lived to be eighty-six, dying in 1937. His Obituary ends with the text: *Blessed are the clean of heart, for they shall see God.* He it was who gave Matt Talbot, whose attendance at school had been so unsatisfactory, the only formal education he got.

Since the publication of earlier editions of this book, further details regarding the Talbot boys' schooling have been discovered. Matt Talbot was first enrolled in St Laurence O'Toole's Christian Brothers' School on July 8th, 1864; his address was given as Newcomen Court; Father's occupation—cooper. He left in June 1865. Opposite the date of leaving, the observation; "Remained at home through necessity" was entered in roll. John Talbot attended this school from August 1863 to January 1866. The comment: "Remained at home on account of his father's illness," which was entered opposite date of leaving, was later altered to "Sent to Room 2." (Room 2 was for more advanced pupils). Robert Talbot also attended St Laurence's for about two months in the end of 1866.

CHAPTER III

WHEN HE LEFT SCHOOL IN THE SUMMER OF 1868, at the age of twelve, Matt Talbot got his first job. He was a messenger-boy with the firm of E. and J. Burke, Ltd., in the North Lotts, wine merchants who also did bottling for Guinness's Brewery and were agents to William Younger and Company, the Edinburgh brewers. They had offices both at 16 Bachelor's Walk and at 59 Abbey Street; in the lane running between these main-street addresses, North Lotts, they had stores: No. 15 and Nos 43 to 46 inclusive. An old employee who died several years ago remembered young Talbot "and could not say much to his credit concerning his time in the North Lotts bottling stores."

He went to work as a messenger for the Port and Docks Board on September 1st, 1872. He is entered in the books as receiving boy's wages of 6s. a week from that date, so he must have been with Messrs Burke for about four years. He remained with the Port and Docks Board until April 24th, 1874, which is the last date on which there is an entry for "Boy's Wages, 6s." as having been paid to Matt Talbot.

In her evidence given before the 1931 Tribunal, Matt Talbot's sister, Mary (Mrs Andrews) stated:

> Even before his conversion Matt had good points; he was very straight and honourable; free from all deception; pure-minded; though he did curse and profane the Holy Name, we used to remark that he did not use impure language and would have nothing to do with women. He

never missed Mass in those days, even though he might have gone to bed drunk on the Saturday night. Neither did he ever speak disrespectfully of religion and he was always very devout to Our Lady. If he neglected his morning prayers, he would never omit to bless himself when going out the door. Even then Matt had the desire to be a good man, but the company was too much for him. I do not think he went to the sacraments, though he went to the mission during Lent. All his wages went to the public-house. Prior to his conversion he was, on a couple of occasions away from home for short periods; the longest time he spent away was five or six months when he was on a building job.

Matt began to work when about twelve and, in his first job—at a bottling stores—learned to take alcoholic drink to excess. My father saw this, gave him a severe thrashing and found a new situation for him as a messenger boy in the Port and Docks Board Office. But he continued to drink notwithstanding all my father did to cure him. Matt left his job after three years so as not to bring disgrace on his father who was employed by the Port and Docks Board. He then became a bricklayer's labourer, but continued his drinking habits; though he aways worked very hard all his wages went in drink—he even pawned his boots to buy drink. He often missed his Easter Duty in those years, but was always careful about Sunday Mass; he said few prayers. His companions were all men; he had no women or girl friends and there was never anything against his moral character.

Mrs Susan Fylan, another sister of Matt Talbot's, corroborated Mrs Andrew's evidence and added further details:

He told me himself that he sold his boots and shirt to get drink, and he used to get drink on credit, often having his wages spent in advance. He was quiet when drunk, but used to curse and swear; he used to come home and lie down; drunkenness his only vice; he was hot-tempered and when drunk used to have rows and fights; but ordinarily he was quiet and was not cross with us at home. He was also strictly honest. I heard him say (after his conversion) that even when drinking he was devout in his mind to the Blessed Virgin and used to say an odd *Hail Mary,* and he attributed his conversion to this.

When interviewed in the end of 1952 both Pat Doyle, the very old man already mentioned, and Thomas Ward, the clerk of St Agatha's Church, made statements that conflict on one point with the evidence of Mrs Andrews; Pat Doyle said that "Matt and all of them had the liking for drink from the father. John was the best of them; he was a great scholar." (Even though his stay in O'Connell School was short, John Talbot seems to have made rapid strides there and got quick promotion). "They were all impudent when they had a drop in; and it was easy for them to get it on account of working in the Bonded Stores at the Custom House Docks. They used to have a can of it in a bag sometimes; old Talbot (Charles, Matt's father) had a powerful voice; you'd hear him shouting out the men's names; for a while he had a livery and tall hat, but it was John had that after a bit." The Port and Docks Records show that John was an official messenger wearing uniform from 1870 onwards. Mr Ward stated that Matt's father "was often drunk on a Saturday and very quarrelsome too when he had drink in."

Pat Doyle's reminiscences of the life of the Talbots and their friends and neighbours of the North Strand area in the later 'seventies and early 'eighties are worth giving verbatim.*

---

* Pat Doyle was not a witness at either Process. His statements are not sworn evidence but were taken down by the author in 1953.

One time they (the Talbots) were in a house with a garden; you could see it from the canal. There was a quarry opposite the Ivy Church on the North Strand. It used to be filled with rubbish. There were always old grannies and children picking cinders there; it was the children who got the most cinders; the grannies would be looking for empty bottles; you could sell them for the price of a drink. Drink was cheap then—tuppence for a pint of porter and whiskey at thruppence halfpenny a glass. You could sell empty bottles at Fletcher's of North William Street, a drink and provisions shop; if you brought in a sack of empties, they'd give you half gallon of porter in a can, and the loan of the can and a couple of tumblers. Publicans nowadays wouldn't trust you like that.

There used to be a *shebeen* in Maggie Kavanagh's in Great Britain Street (now Parnell Street); that used to be a great place for the crowd coming from picking the cinders. Maggie was well able to drink herself. She used to have pigs'cheeks in barrels of brine. Matt Talbot and 'the Man' (Phil Talbot) and meself used to go to Maggie's *shebeen* often. When we had no luck with bottles, or no way of getting the money for the drink, we used to steal a pig's cheek and go sell it, God forgive us, and come back and buy the drink off Maggie—with the money we got for the pig's cheek belonging to herself. When we'd plan to make a raid on the barrel, some of the lads would keep Maggie talking, the rest would stand in front of the fellow edging back to the barrel; he'd slip the pig's cheek under his coat and duck out.

A queer thing—Matt would never steal a pig's cheek. He always got out of it, when it would be his turn. But he wouldn't refuse the drink after the fellow who did the stealing and the selling came back with the money. Matt was a coward that way; and in other ways too; he never would go in swimming up above Annesley Bridge on hot days when all of us would be going in; he was too fearful; we all called him a coward. Maybe he wasn't one, but we called him one. I often stole pigs' cheeks from Maggie Kavanagh, God forgive me! I remember I had a navy blue coat, and from having the brine—the pigs' cheeks used to be dripping with it, you understand, lifting them out of the barrel—having this so often buttoned in against me chest, all the dye ran out of me coat. Me mother said to me, 'That's a queer thing, Pat, after I paying four shillings for that coat at the Daisy Market.'

That's where we used to buy our clothes: at the Daisy Market. The gentry's gentlemen used to sell their old uniforms the minute they got a little worn; some of them wouldn't have a *breac* on them.

I remember one Saturday night I got a trousers for one and eight-pence, a dress-coat for tenpence—oh, that was a powerful bargain! and a brown hat for fourpence. I was working at the time for a man by the name of Poole. Matt was working for him, for a bit. This Mr Poole and another named Bryans were building a skittle-alley out at Clontarf; the skittles were banished out there, when the nuns came; it was too near to the convent. Mr Poole was a bit lame, but he was a well-connected man. When I went out that Monday morning to work with me new clothes on me—the bargains I got, or, rather, that me mother got—because she was a great woman to buy—Mr Poole took one look at me and says he to me: 'Is it to a ball or to building you're going, Pat Doyle?' And I got the sack on the spot. I must have been lookin' a bit of a swell, all right, with me swallow-tail coat and me brown derby hat. But there were no Unions in those days. You could be sacked for nothing.

But I was telling you about Matt and how we used to steal the pigs' cheeks for the drink. John Talbot would never come with us, but Bob would be there; later he married and was living in Little Britain Street. He was a great man but wild; they were all wild but John. Phil, 'the Man' was the wildest of them; Joe was the only big fellow in the family; they were all terribly small, only Joe; and the father was very small.

Sometimes we used to go to Rosie Plunkett's; Rosie was a washer-woman and 'tis she'd be glad when anyone would give her a hand turning the mangle. She used to do a lot of washing for the soldiers in the barracks—Aldborough Barracks. There was full and plenty in that barracks, because the Quarter-Masters were all billeted there. Often they'd give away pigs' cheeks for nothing; not out of charity but because they'd have ordered too much and wouldn't want it to be lying about when the high-up officers would be going round inspecting. Old grannies with sons in the soldiers used to go up there to get free pigs' heads; but Rosie Plunkett, on account of doing the washing, would get as many pigs' heads as she could carry home—along with her bit of pay for the washing, you understand. She used to sell the pigs' heads a little less than shop price; they used to cost ninepence or tenpence in the shops then, but Rosie would sell them for sevenpence or eightpence. (Times are different now; I saw one in a shop in Talbot Street for ten shillings one day last year!). The 'Man' Talbot (Phil) and meself and Matt—but Matt was older than us—used to turn the mangle for Rosie; and she'd give us a pig's cheek in return; she was a decent woman, Rosie. Then we'd sell it and drink the price of it.

Times are changed. There used be wrestling matches in Fren's(?) Gardens, near Ballybough Road. And in the summer evenings, and on Sundays, the young fellows would play Common (caman?)—hurling they call it now; our coats would do us for the goal-posts; we'd place them on the ground with stones on them. Sometimes the priests would come round to the houses and for a while we'd all go once or twice a week to the Convent in William Street, where the nuns would have classes in prayers and catechism for youngsters who hadn't much schooling. They used to give prizes of sweets and toys to small children; but big lads, if they were any good at the classes, would get what the nuns used to call Premiums—framed religious pictures, rosary beads and the like. And Father Young, the holy man, used to be hunting up children and young fellows to go learn the Catechism.

Matt's father, Charlie, was a shocking man when he had the drop in; he'd kick the shins from under you; and he'd roar and shout something terrible. There was one of the boys called Charlie, too, but he didn't live long; he had a stand near Amiens Street Station and he used to be polishing shoes for people in the street. Phil was very small; 'twas he was the impudent lad! Bob Talbot wasn't long married when he died; 'the Man'—Phil—and meself went to his wake on a Sunday evening; I remember it well, in Little Britain Street (now Parnell Street).

But as for Matt; he was a good hodman; everyone had to give him the palm for that. When he was with Pemberton's, the builders, he'd do more in half-an-hour than the rest would in an hour. The Master Builder, or the Foreman, used to put him in front to make the rest of the men keep up with him. Mary, the eldest girl, married a man named Courtney, but she wasn't so young when she got married.

Another place where we often went drinking was at Hunter's—a little grocery place off Love Lane; they hadn't any licence. I'll say this for Matt: though he was very fond of the drink, I never heard him cursing or swearing. He'd go to Mass, but he was no way religious in those days. He only wanted one thing—the drink; he'd never bother with parties or dancing or a game of cards; even when the rest of us would be going he wouldn't come. Outside the

College on Clonliffe Road there would be games going on during bright summer evenings, but he'd never come; not even to look on. Some of the boys, young men they were, not chaps, used to twist the ropes for the girls to skip. The Reverend gentlemen in the College were a bit 'down' on that and there was a queer running, I can tell you, if any of them came out. Matt wouldn't join in the skipping either, though 'twas harmless fun. But he'd do anything for the drink. He'd think nothing of walking out to Baldoyle to hold horses for an evening; and he often held horses for hours outside Carolan's pub on the Howth Road. That's what Matt would be at while we'd be at the wrestling or the cards; ah, he was a bit of a granny in those days. And we used to tell him that, too. He'd come back with a half-gallon of porter after his evening holding the horses; we would all help him to drink it. Everyone drank in those days, even the children; when the porter would be going the rounds they'd all have to get their half-gill. Ah, it's changed times!

Thomas Ward of St Agatha's, being a decade younger than Pat Doyle, cannot recall any incidents in which Matt figured during those years; his memories are all of the younger Talbots, at the age of seven or eight, when they played the favourite game of the small boys of the Dublin of that time—"Hunt-the-Cap." But he has vivid memories of the "Man" Talbot, Phil, seldom sober, often heralding his approach with shouts and "roaring songs."

It will be remembered how, in 1874, the Talbots moved to 5, Love Lane, Ballybough where their accommodation was the worst of any encountered in their many changes of address. By the time John was twenty, Matt eighteen and Bob sixteen; they—and possibly Joseph and the oldest girl, Mary, then fourteen—would have been all working.

The logical explanation for the increased poverty of the family is that most of the earnings went on drink.

Father Mathew was not twenty years dead. Memories still lingered of the time he preached in Sandyford in 1840, giving the pledge to 20,000; and of the open-air platform erected outside the Custom House that same year, when 25,000 people came, in batches of 5,000, to take the pledge In one year, 1840, 173,000 people in Dublin alone took the pledge from the great Capuchin who, in that year, made three visits to the metropolis. Writing to Father Mathew in November, 1840, Archbishop Murray stated that

> while vast benefits had been produced by the pledge, the publicans had sustained little injury. They re-opened their shops for the sale of clothes, Irish manufactures and other such articles, and one business supplied the place of the other. The largest prison in Dublin was closed for want of prisoners.

In 1841 a great St Patrick's Day Total Abstinence Procession was held in the Fifteen Acres, Phoenix Park, in which an estimated quarter of a million people participated; the band of St Paul's Temperance Society, Arran Quay, was seated on a dray drawn by six horses, while the blue-and-gold-uniformed Father Matthew band reached, four abreast, from Mary's Abbey to the present Mellowes Bridge. From that until the end of the Crimean War the Temperance movement was strong in Dublin.

But when Father Mathew died, the life of his great crusade seemed to die with him. His preaching-power, his magnetic personality, engendered tremendous enthusiasm in his hearers, who saw in him a zeal and self-denial that could not be hidden. The vitality of the Temperance revival emanating from the great Apostle of Temperance, depended in great part on the man himself. "Within a decade of the founder's death," writes Dr Rodgers in his *Father Theobald Mathew,* "the movement appeared moribund." And again: "Of the five millions of the Irish people who had taken the pledge, only some hundred thousand remained faithful."

In the post-Crimean period drunkenness increased everywhere in Ireland. The English authorities, having assessed the worthlessness as citizens of the first lot of foreigners to arrive in London after the war had ended, hastily arranged that all further batches of such undesirables should be diverted to Dublin. Already well-studded with military barracks, each holding more than its quota of Queen's soldiers, the Irish capital was now made the dumping-ground for the riff-raff of Europe. The latter were no advocates of temperance; neither were the garrison troops. In the early 1860's over 1,500 licensed premises—and, presumably, almost as many unlicensed—were doing good business with Dublin's 250,000 people. The arrests for drunkenness in the city for 1865 numbered 16,192, one-third of those arrested being women. Deaths for intoxication were on the increase; in 1862 there were four, in 1863 six, in 1864 fourteen, in 1865 twelve, and in 1866 nineteen deaths from over-indulgence in drink.

Dr Yore of Arran Quay, Dr Spratt of Clarendon Street, Fr Meehan of SS. Michael and John's, Fr Ignatius of Mount Argus, and others, conducted, each in his own way, zealous and successful campaigns against the spread of intemperance. The saintly Father Henry Young preached and wrote treatises with the object of promoting temperance and stemming many of the abuses that had arisen. It was an accepted system that workmen were paid on Saturdays at the public-house, either in cash or by cheque or order to be cashed by the publican—it being taken for granted by the latter that, for the service rendered in allowing such financial transactions to take place on his premises and at the cost of his time and trouble, the workmen thus obliged would spend a good deal of their earnings before leaving the publichouse.

Father Young wrote:

> It would be desirable ... if employers were brought to a sense of their duty and obliged to pay their workmen in their own house or in the workshop, or at a fixed, proper and convenient place where no drink should be allowed.

But the workmen were not the only citizens of Dublin addicted to heavy drinking. Thackeray, in his *Irish Sketch-Book*, told of how he had been wined and dined in Dublin. At Mr Lovegrove's the main course was lobster, which was shelled, coated with a mixture of mustard, vinegar, catsup and strong cayenne pepper.

> and cooked in an affair called a *dispatcher*, over whiskey; a glass and a half of sherry was added to the pan; the lobster was served hot and eaten on the spot. Porter is commonly drunk with this and whiskey punch afterwards and the dish is fit for an emperor.

Other drinks followed until "the claret began to have a rather mawkish taste, so whiskey and water was ordered ..." But the night was not yet over ...

> At Kildare Street we had white neck-cloths, black waiters, wax-candles and some of the best wine in Europe; at Mr —————'s, the publisher's, wax-candles and some of the best wine in Europe; at Mr Lever's,

wax-candles and some of the best wine in Europe; at Trinity College—but there is no need to mention what took place at Trinity College ...I am sure if the Fellows of T.C.D. only drank beer at dinner they would not believe *that* ....

The Irish Bishops issued several Pastorals on Temperance. There was a controversy about the nature of the temperance pledge between Frederick Lucas, the distinguished convert, editor of the London *Tablet,* and Father Mathew; coupled with the fact that Lucas afterwards became an ardent supporter of the Fenians. this gave rise to a tendency to identify temperance with anti-nationalism, or, at least, with something not altogether Catholic, Maynooth and several Bishops having taken the side of Lucas in his disagreement with Father Mathew.

Mrs Annie Johnson (née Andrews) daughter of Christopher Andrews and Mary Talbot, the oldest of Matt's sisters, gave the following evidence at the 1948 Enquiry regarding Matt Talbot's drinking habits:

> I heard from my mother (Mary Talbot), my grandmother (Matt's mother) and Mrs Fylan (Matt's sister Susan) that Matt used to drink at an early age, and they told me how he used to come home on a Saturday night and hand his mother a shilling (it was all he had left out of his week's wages), and say: "Here, mother, is that any good to you?" His mother used to say: "God forgive you, Matt. Is that the way to treat your mother?"
>
> I heard that he was always a good workman ... He owed money for drink; he used to get drink on credit ... Some time before his conversion he and his brothers stole a violin from a fiddler and sold it for drink ...

Matt Talbot, in later years, was hardly ever heard to

refer to his life at this period. One Tribunal witness, Mr Francis Donnelan, who lived in the same house as Matt for sixteen years before the latter's death, stated.

> He said to me that he was not highly educated ...Matt admitted to me that he was fond of drink in his younger days; he said he was "careless about his religion." Sometime after World War I, about 1919 or 1920, while I was on strike, he came to see me one day; we had some conversation about religion and he asked me if I ever read religious books. He said to me: "I should be the last person to advise anyone about religion, because when I was young I was very careless about religion because of drink, and I broke my mother's heart." ...He was accustomed to spend all his wages on drink and sometimes came home in his bare feet on a Saturday night. ...

From his early 'teens unitl his late twenties, the pattern of Matt Talbot's life was that of the drunkard, lost to self respect, deaf to the appeals of his mother, a slave to the craving for alcohol, a workman who in his hours of leisure drank not only his earnings, but any other money he or his drinking companions could come by, honestly or otherwise.

CHAPTER IV

IN A VISITORS'S BOOK, KEPT BY THE LATE MRS
Susan Purcell in her Religious Repository in Granby
Lane, there was an entry:

> I, Catherine Carrick, gave Matt Tlbot his last pint of
> porter before taking the life pledge. I was then Catherine
> Kelly, living at 30 Strandville Avenue, North Strand. He
> came back to me in the shop; he told me he would never
> touch drink for his life.

Mrs Carrick did not give the approximate date of this,
for Matt, momentous occasion. The evidence of others
makes the date rather indefinite. Mrs Johnston, Matt's
niece, testified:

> Matt had been away from work for some days and had
> no money left; on the Saturday, he went down with his
> brothers, Philip and Joseph, to wait at the
> public-house—O'Meara's, I think—on the North Strand,
> when the men were coming home from work. His friends
> passed him by without asking him in for a drink, and Matt
> said to his brother Joe, "I am going home." When he
> reached home, his mother opened the door and said:
> "Matt, you are home early"; he then said, "I am going up
> to Holy Cross College to take the pledge." His mother
> said: "If you don't intend to keep it, don't take it." 'He
> went to the College, where he took the pledge for six
> months; later, he renewed the pledge for life. When he
> took the pledge he began praying and used to go, secretly,
> in the evening to a church. In the beginning he was
> ashamed to be seen going to the church; he used to visit
> different churches in the evening, including St Joseph's,
> Berkeley Road. His conversion took place about the time
> of my mother's marriage, in the year 1882.

Mrs Johnson's evidence is substantially the same as that which her mother, Mrs Andrews, gave at the first Enquiry, twenty years earlier. Mrs Andrews stated then that Matt had been away from work because he was drinking. She also said that he stood at the corner of William Street and the North Strand; her account runs:

My mother said "You're home early, Matt, and you're sober!" He replied, "Yes, mother, I am." After dinner he remained in the house, which was not usual, and finally he remarked to my mother "I'm going to take the pledge." She smiled and said, "Go, in God's name, but don't take it unless you are going to keep it." He said, "I'll go, in God's name." As he was going out mother said, "God give you strength to keep it." He went to Clonliffe, made his Confession, and took the pledge for three months. He had been a couple of years away from the Sacraments then. Next morning—Sunday—he went to Holy Communion. On Monday he went to 5 a.m. Mass in Gardiner Street and was at his work as usual at 6 a.m. This he made a regular practice of from that on; but after his work, to keep away from his companions, he used to walk to a distant church, either St Joseph's, Berkeley Road, or St Peter's, Phibsboro', and remain there until bedtime. Once or twice —possibly on a Saturday—he went with the men to the public-house, but he drank only minerals, and he usually spent Saturday afternoons away from where he might meet his old companions, and generally in a church. He had a bad time of it at first and sometimes said to my mother that, when the three months were up, he would drink again.

Mrs Fylan's account of the incidents leading up to the conversion agreed with the foregoing, but she added:

He was a changed man immediately after taking the pledge. We never heard him swear again. He put two pins in the cuff of his coat to check any temptation to swear ...His workmates were astonished when they heard of Matt taking the pledge; and they were still more astonished when he kept it.

Sir Joseph Glynn, in his *Life of Matt Talbot,* fixes the date of Matt's conversion at approximately 1884. Mrs Andrews told him that Matt took the pledge two years after her own marriage in 1882. He adds these details:

> Matt always stated that he took the total abstinence pledge from the Rev. Dr Keane at Clonliffe College. It is not easy to reconcile this statement with the dates. The Rev. Dr Keane was a Professor in Clonliffe College until 1879, when, at his request, he was transferred to a curacy in St Michan's parish. He remained in St Michan's until some time in 1883, when he joined the Dominican Order. Matt took the pledge in 1884, though the time of the year is not known .... Dr Keane was a constant visitor in Clonliffe College during the years he was a curate in St Michan's, and it is possible that he met Matt Talbot there on the Saturday afternoon in question and administered the pledge. It is, of course, quite possible that Matt made a mistake in the identity of the priest who heard his confession and administered the pledge, though this is very difficult to imagine because Dr Keane was a very well-known man in the public life of the country during these years and his name must have been familiar to all Dublin working-men.

Enquiries in Clonliffe and at the Dominican Novitiate at Tallaght, show that Dr Keane, although his curacy at St Michan's terminated at Christmas 1883, did not enter at Tallaght until June 1884; so, having been formerly on the staff at Clonliffe, it is reasonable to conclude that he stayed there for six months before he left the secular for the regular clergy.

Pat Doyle had some useful and amusing reminiscences to supply at this juncture. In an interview he stated:

On the morning after the Park Murders, in May 1882,[*] there was terrible activity in the city; the police and the soldiers were searching everywhere; our part of the city most of all. Me father and meself and others, plenty others, had no wish to be questioned by them boyos: I'm not saying, now, that we had hand, act or part in what happened; nor even that we knew anything; but we had our own reasons for getting out and getting a good bit away from Dublin that morning. So off we went, a crowd of us, down to Mayo, where we got work under the Congested Districts Board building Cleggan Pier. I was never down in that part of the country before, and I found it very strange at first.

Up to the time I left Dublin for Mayo, Matt used to be out drinking every time he had the price of it, with Phil and Joe and meself. "Barney"—that was a nickname we had for Matt round Newcomen Avenue—was a hard man for the drink. Well, I was down in the West for a long time, for a couple of years anyway. The while in the country made me a bit lonesome or something, because, when I came back I was going around looking for all the old pals, or looking for a fight—I was always fond of the scrapping. "Where's Barney?" I used to ask the lads—meaning Matt Talbot. "O, Barney's a changed man," they used to say and leave it at that. But I didn't believe them. Then one evening I was in great fettle, having had a fight down at the docks the night before and beaten a big navvy, twice me size; I was coming along up the North Circular, when someone says to me: "There's Barney now, Doyle. Weren't you asking about him?"

* Lord Frederick Cavendish, the Chief Secretary, and Mr Thomas Burke, Under-Secretary, were stabbed to death while walking in the Pheonix Park on May 6th, 1882.

Sure enough, there was Matt. And wasn't *he* looking for *me*. So off we went together.

"So you're at it again?" says he to me. And that was the way he saluted me after me two years and more away!

"At what?" says I, letting on I didn't know what he was driving at.

"At the fighting," Matt says.

"And why wouldn't I?" I asks him.

"Give it up, Pat give it up," says he. By this time we had reached Fallon's pub—at the corner of the North Circular Road and Margaret Place.

"Come on in with me," I said.

"No," said he. "You go on in, get one glass of whiskey and then come on with me."

"Come where?" I asked him.

"Get your glass of whiskey and come on," he ordered me, in the way he had of speaking—abrupt like—he never had much to say. I thought that he didn't want to go into Fallon's, that he might be owing money or something there. So I went in and had the one drink and came out again and there was Matt waiting for me. And I forgot to ask him where he wanted me to go as the two of us began to talk about old times and all the changes during the years I was down in the West, and I began telling him about the time I had of it at the building of the Safety Pier and, however it was, I never noticed where we were walking until he had me in the grounds of Holy Cross College. There was a Reverend gentleman walking up and down reading his book. He seemed to know Matt well and Matt knew him.

"Here he is for you now, Father", said he. "I brought him up to take the pledge," and before I could say a word there I was down on me knees taking the pledge. And that wasn't all of it; before I could get up, or reach over for me hat that I had tossed on the grass, Matt says:

"As you have him now, Father, make him go to his duty."

That was too much for me. I made a grab at the hat, and I missed it; but, before another word was said by one or other of them, I jumped up and cleared off as fast as ever I could—leaving me hat on the grass in Clonliffe College grounds. Matt was very vexed with me for running off like that. I didn't meet him for a long time after that—nor didn't want to meet him, I can tell you; I heard he didn't like it, the way I ran off on himself and the Reverend gentleman in Clonliffe College.

Pat Doyle's story indicates that Matt was used to calling on the priest to whom he brought his friend. The anecdote would also seem to show that Matt was then but in th first stages of conversion, his zealous efforts to woo a boon companion of his drinking-days not only to temperance but to the better life, being more in the tradition of the newly-converted than of a soul who, consolidated in virtue, has learned to temper zeal with prudence and patience.

The conversion of Matt Talbot began somewhere between North Strand Road and his home on that afternoon, when, smarting at the treatment he had received from those whom he thought his friends, he suddenly resolved to turn to Him Who does not fail.

Each conversion, wrote Father Faber, and there are thousands daily, is a divine work of art, standing by itself, each in its own way being a heavenly masterpiece ...A man goes forth into the streets in a state of mortal sin ...In the streets he meets, perhaps, a funeral, a priest, or he comes across a priest by whose demeanour he perceives that he has the Blessed Sacrament with him. Thoughts crowd into his mind. Faith is awake and on the watch. Grace disposes him for grace. The veil falls from sin; and he turns from the hideous vision with shame, with detestation, with humility. The eye of his soul glances to his crucified Redeemer. Fear has led the way for hope, and hope has the heart to resolve, and faith tells him that his resolution will be accepted, and he loves—how can he help loving Him Who will accept so poor a resolution? There is a pressure on his soul. It is less than the sting of a bee, even if it hurts at all. Yet it was the pressure of the Creator, omnipotent, immense, all-holy and incomprehensible, on his living soul. The unseen hand was laid on him only for a moment. He has not passed half-a-dozen shop fronts, and the work is done. He is contrite. Hell is vanquished. All the angels of heaven are in a stir of joy. God is yearning over his soul with love and ineffable desire ...

That passage might have been written to describe the change of heart wrought in Matt Talbot on the—for him—wonderful Saturday, sometime in the early months of 1884. Outwardly he was probably little changed; a small wiry man, with the same rather irascible temperament, the same inherited tendency to shout and bluster like his father, to work hard like his mother; his education was still of the most rudimentary nature—gentle Brother Kelly's lessons hardly more than a blurred memory. He retained that pugnacity which was a Talbot characteristic. He was still a builder's labourer. But he was more. He had also begun work with another Builder, helping to rear on the newly-cleared site of his soul, an edifice whose length and breadth and height and depth was not his to gauge, whose spires he might not lift his head to admire; his spiritual life was, like his temporal life, that of the unskilled labourer, the hod-carrier. But he had always been a good workman; neither did he change in this; before his conversion men had called him "the best hodman in Dublin"; the foreman put him in front to set the pace for the others. So might the angels have spoken of his work on building that tabernacle not made with hands; "the best workman in Dublin; put in front to set the pace."

Matt Talbot was then nearing thirty; ahead of him stretched forty years. Before considering how he spent the years between 1885 and 1925, it is time to look again at his environment, his city, his times.

Cardinal Cullen died in 1878, Cardinal McCabe, his successor, in 1885. The next archbishop was Dr Walsh, the President of Maynooth College. The memory of the saintly Father Henry Young, who died in 1867, not a stone's throw from the North Strand area, was still fresh in the Pro-Cathedral and St Agatha's parishes. Other great priests had come and gone. Dead was the benevolent Dr Yore of Arran Quay, the great advocate of temperance—the man who sold his own library to found the Catholic Institution for the Deaf and Dumb, and the Asylum for Catholic Blind. The venerable Father Haly, S.J., died in 1882, in his 87th year. "One shake of Father Haly's white head did more good than three or four sermons," his congregation said; but Gardiner Street pulpit knew him no more. The gifted Irish Dominican, Father Tom Burke, whose preaching in Rome and England and America, as in his native land, drew immense crowds of every strata of society, non-Catholics as well as Catholics, died in 1883. His eloquence and intellect and magnetic personality were at the disposal of every good cause; his immense popularity—a danger to a lesser man—was to him but another talent, to be turned to good account in the service of God. His power over his hearers came as much from what he was as from what he said; it was typical of him that he rose from his sick-bed to preach a charity sermon in the Jesuit Church of St Francis Xavier eight days before his death. Though he had, literally, to drag himself into the pulpit, he pleaded the cause of 5,000 famine-stricken children in Donegal with tremendous ardour. "He had gathered," wrote Justice O'Hagen, who was in the congregation, "what remains of life and fire were left within him, to do this last act of charity and pity." One wonders if Matt Talbot ever heard the great Dominican preach on Temperance; it was a favourite theme of Fr Burke's and one to which he returned again and again.

After the assassination of Lord Cavendish and Mr Burke in the Phoenix Park in May 1882, there was a great outcry—led by Castle Society—against the Invincibles. But, if the same outcry had been raised against police attacks on the citizens, a year earlier, the Invincible movement might not have sprung up as it did, almost over-night, among a population maddened by brutal police attacks on public meetings of all kinds. After Parnell's arrest in October, 1881, the *Weekly Irish Times* describes how the police attacked a peaceable meeting in O'Connell Street:

> Their conduct was such as to appear almost incredible to all who had been witness to it...After every charge they made, men—amongst them respectable citizens—were left lying in the streets, blood pouring from the wounds they received on the heads from the batons of the police, while others were covered with severe bruises from the kicks and blows of clenched fists delivered with all the strength that powerful men could exert.

The *Irish Times,* commenting on a further exhibition of police brutality in 1881, said:

The police drew their batons, and the scene which followed beggars description. Charging headlong into the people, the constables struck right and left, and men and women fell under their blows ... No quarter was given The roadway was strewn with the bodies of people. From the Ballast Office to the Bridge, from the Bridge to Sackville Street, the charge was continued with fury. Women fled shrieking, and their cries rendered even more painful the scene of barbarity which was being enacted. All was confusion, and naught could be seen but the police mercilessly batoning the public ...As an instance of the conduct of the police, it may be mentioned that ... more than a dozen students of Trinity College and a militia officer—unoffending passers-by—were knocked down and kicked, and two postal telegram messengers, engaged in carrying telegrams, were barbarously assailed. When the people were felled, they were kicked on the ground and when they rose again, they were again knocked down by any constable who met them.

But, splendidly remote and supremely indifferent to the citizens being laid low by "Buckshot" Forster's peelers, the Castle set lived "the life of Reilly."

The Countess of Fingall, in her memoirs, *Seventy Years Young,* recalls the early 'eighties, when she was a beautiful debutante, attending the State Balls, Drawing-Rooms and Levees; she describes being presented to Their Excellencies:

There was a crowd about the gates of the Castle. The Dublin poor always turned out to see any sight that there was. They shivered on the pavement in their thin, ragged clothes, waiting for hours sometimes, so that they might see the ladies in their silks and satins and furs step from their carriages into the warmth and light and gaiety that received them. The poor were incredibly patient. Even then I was dimly aware of that appalling contrast between their lives and ours, and wondered how long they would remain patient ...

The mounted orderlies went riding, through the streets of Dublin, delivering invitation for the Castle Balls and Parties, such eagerly-awaited invitations ... In those days of little traffic, one could hear a horse coming at the other end of the (Merrion) Square ... The windows of the bedrooms look out on an appalling slum ... But the windows are curtained, and one need not lift the curtains, and the wailing voice of a weary child only comes faintly through the glass. There is waltz music to drown it ... The times were troubled, I realised, and Lord Spenser rode sadly through the streets of Dublin with his escort about him for protection ....Since the Phoenix Park murders, of course, there was always great alarm about the safety of the Lord Lieutenant.

Servants of the gentry who revolved about the Lord Lieutenant, have recorded their memories of the Dublin of that time. In 1957 an old man of eighty-five gave a press interview on the Dublin of his boyhood. He began to work in 1885 at the age of thirteen.

I was a page-boy for the people in Mountjoy Square. The butlers blew a whistle and shouted for "Tommy," and I'd be sent down to the Post Office to collect letters, or go to the Bank for money. The banks paid in gold, and I'd carry back the sovereigns in a little bag of leather, tied with a draw-string.

The Earl of Glencarty lived in No. 1, Miss Lawless, the last of the old aristocrats, lived in No. 2 ...The Royal Hunt used to meet in the Square and with horses and hounds move off down Belvedere Place. As a page-boy, dressed in a livery given me by the Earl of Meath (who resided in Nos. 4, 5, 6 and 7) I had the duty of hooking up the long dresses of Lily Langtry, "the Jersey Lily," the most beautiful woman in the world .... There was a man named Rogers who had hacking stables in Fitzwilliam Street. He dressed me up in leggings and riding breeches. In those days the people who lived in Mountjoy Square would not drive or ride into the city until the refuse had been swept from the streets. There was even a special inspection of the drains in Mountjoy Square every day. They used to take away the sewage and dump it in the sloblands, and there was an epidemic and the place had to be sprayed with creosote.

The sloblands referred to were just beyond the North Strand area where the Talbots lived. There is little recorded about the Talbots in the early 'eighties. Just six months before being retired altogether by the Port and Docks authorities, Charles Talbot received belated promotion; he was paid "under-foreman's wages" of 21s. a week. On February 2nd, 1882, he retired on six-and-eightpence a week pension; the pension was increased to 10s. a week in November, 1884. He was just turned sixty. John, thirty, was in steady employment in the Port and Docks. Matt was twenty-eight, Bob twenty-six, Joe somewhat younger, Phil twenty, and the youngest, Charlie, about eleven. Mary, twenty-four, was married; Elizabeth was seventeen, and Susan thirteen. Except for John, who may then have been married, the men of the family all had more or less regular employment; but, though they could have lived in comparative comfort, the fact that all were steady drinkers—Matt and Phil heavy drinkers who contributed little or nothing to the household budget—must have kept the family income in a sadly depleted state; and that for many years. At the time of Matt's conversion they were living at 13, Newcomen Avenue North Strand.

From her marriage in 1853 to that Saturday afternoon in the first half of 1884 when her son, Matt, told her he was going to take the pledge, Elizabeth Talbot had seen many a change. She was now to witness a far greater one. It is typical of the woman whose heart Matt later accused himself of having broken, that she told him not to take a pledge if he did not mean to keep it. It is a mark of an uncompromising character. Matt's sisters, Mary and Susan, both of whom were present on that occasion, in later years recorded that she added: "and may God give you the grace to keep it." The prayer was answered far beyond the expectations of the mother who uttered it, or the son to whom it was addressed.

CHAPTER V

VERY LITTLE IS KNOWN OF MATT TALBOT FOR the seven years subsequent to his conversion. It is hardly likely that his case deviated much from the usual pattern of conversion. His family "never heard him swear again." Matt—sober—was a nine-days-wonder to his workmates, whose astonishment increased when, as the months went by, they found that he was deadly in earnest about keeping his pledge. But it is unlikely that anyone—even his own—realised what a complete conversion Matt Talbot's had been. At first, beyond the fact that he kept the pledge, his life, to all appearances, would hardly have shown much trace of the tremendous interior renewal and reorientation that had taken place in early 1884. It is a fundamental spiritual axiom that grace does not change nature; it builds on it. The work accomplished in him on the day of his conversion might be compared to the clearing of a block of derelict, condemned buildings. The site was ready; that which constituted a danger had been removed. But it was the same site, with the same natural advantages, the same drawbacks; the man was the same Matt Talbot, the same "unskilled" labourer, the same unimportant citizen of Dublin of the 'eighties.

Now that the twenty-eight-year-old Matt had found—in one sense at least—permanent employment, he brought to the service of God the same verve and determination and natural tenacity that had always marked him out among his fellow-workers. His one-time drinking companion, Pat Doyle, summing up his character, remarked: "He could never go easy—at anything." When he was working with the builders, the foremen put him first, "to set the pace."

These same natural reserves of energy, the same indomitable will—endowments that hitherto dragged him down—now spurred him in another direction. His spiritual exertions bore a strange analogy to his arduous, daily toil. His calling in life was to fetch and carry for the trained workers who specialised in particular crafts and trades; his constant occupation was the carrying of bricks and mortar, of heavy, hard-to-balance planks. A man bearing a load on his shoulder walks with bowed head, his glance continually on the ground; he is careful to place his feet securely as he mounts ladders to take the measure of passages through which he must manoeuvre awkward loads. Not for him to stand with architect or foreman admiring this facade, superintending that beam swung into position, looking up at the spires beginning to rear their splendour above surrounding roof-tops. From the little that is known of Matt Talbot between the years 1884 and 1891, there emerges a man intent on humbling and hiding himself, a soul mindful of its every step, a toiler attentive to his tasks, diligent and constant in his occupations, spiritual and temporal.

Mary Talbot, Mrs. Andrews, testified regarding her brother Matt's life subsequent to his conversion:

> During his free time (from after his day's work until 10 p.m.) he was never off his knees. I never saw him sit down except some visitor called. He even ate his dinner on his knees. At that time he would take meat a couple of times in the week or eggs for his dinner. During Lent he took nothing only dry bread and cocoa and sometimes a little fish. For June he never took meat, as he fasted in honour of the Sacred Heart. He did similar fasts during a week or more before each big Feast of the Church. He also abstained from meat from the beginning of Advent until

St Stephen's Day in honour of the Infant Saviour. And he fasted on all the big Feasts. He slept on a broad plank, the width of his bed, and he had a solid lump of wood for a pillow. He had these covered with a sheet and a light blanket.

Mrs Fylan, Susan Talbot, in her evidence stated that she first noted the plank about 1888.

> When Matt returned for a time to our parents' house he brought the plank and the block with him. When I saw them first they were lying up against the wall. When I asked him what they were for he said, "They're for a purpose." When I saw him praying during the day he sometimes had his arms crossed on his breast. But I very seldom saw him at his real devotions as he wanted to be alone at them ... I bought chains for him several times; he would not say what they were for, but I knew. He would not eat any dainties I put before him.

Less mortified mortals should find some consolation in a further detail Mrs Fylan gave:

> On Christmas morning he would give me special orders to have a bit of tender steak and to fry it for him. He used to be delighted to get that bit of steak on Christmas morning after fasting all Advent ....
>
> ... But usually he lived practically on dry bread, and shell-cocoa without milk or sugar. One pound of sugar used to do him six months ...He often referred to his past sins and said, "Where would I be only for God and His Blessed Mother?" I often saw Matt with a chisel and hammer chipping his wooden pillow. I think he did that to make it rough and unconfortable. The plank he slept on was rough and unplaned.

The following evidence was given by Matt's niece, Mrs Johnson:

When he took the pledge he began praying and used to go, secretly, in the evenings, to a church; he used to visit different churches in the evening, including St Joseph's, Berkeley Road .... About this time he began to go to Mass daily; he used to go to Mass in Gardiner Street, where there was a special early Mass about six o'clock. After his conversion, he continued with his usual work, and he was very generous with the money he earned. I know that he gave my parents considerable sums of money. My father was often out of work owing to the nature of his occupation and my mother used to go to Matt for help. He always gave what he could and would never take it back; he would say: "Keep it—buy something for the children." Sometime after his conversion he left home because his brothers continued to drink, in spite of his efforts to reform them; he took a room somewhere in Gloucester Street.

It was about 1900 when Matt Talbot went to Gloucester Street, according to the records of the Franciscan Friary, Merchants' Quay, where he was a member of the Third Order. Before he moved to that address, he had been with the family at 12 or 13 Spencer Avenue for a while; he was in his parents' home at Newcomen Avenue about 1894; he had a room in Upper Buckingham Street in 1896 and soon afterwards rejoined his parents who had then left Newcomen Avenue for Middle Gardiner Street.

It is not certain that Matt Talbot had a spiritual director in the years between 1884 and 1891. Later on he had as regular confessor, Dr Hickey, who returned from Rome after his Ordination in 1895 and spent almost thirty years as Professor and Rector in Clonliffe College. Witnesses at the Enquiries gave evidence that Matt was sometimes seen at the confessional of Father James Walsh, S.J., Gardiner Street. In his last years he was also seen occasionally waiting for Father Tom Murphy, S.J. Several witnesses averred that Matt went weekly to Confession in Clonliffe. Replying to a query as to whom he might have had as confessor during those ten years, the late Dr Myles Ronan informed the present writer:

> Matt could have gone to Rev. Dr McGrath, who was a Professor in the College in 1884 and the years following. Dr McGrath was the type of man who would be attracted by a character like Matt's. Dr O'Donnell (Professor of Theology) would also have been in Clonliffe at that time; while in Clonliffe he was also Chaplain to Mountjoy Prison and was usually in touch with stragglers calling to the College at all sorts of times from the prison, etc. He, too, would be a man likely to take an interest in such a case as Matt's.

Dublin's Diocesan Seminary, Holy Cross College, Clonliffe, stands on a well-timbered stretch of meadow-land flanking the Tolka. The College was built when Cardinal Cullen was Archbishop and its crypt is the burial-place of that famous prelate. At the time of Matt Talbot's conversion Holy Cross was on the north rim of the city, but houses were being built on all the roads around it. From 1882 to 1886 it had, as Professor of Philosophy, no less a soul than Father Joseph Marmion, later to be known as Dom Columba Marmion, the great Benedictine Abbot who spiritual teachings have encircled the globe and whose Cause has been introduced in Rome. But there is no evidence that the paths of Matt Talbot and his fellow-Dubliner ever crossed, though both were in the same area of the city from early 1884 to late 1886, the critical period when Matt Talbot was on the first stage of his long spiritual odyssey and when Father Marmion was deciding to leave his friends, his post in Clonliffe, and his country, to "seek God" in the way to which he had been drawn.

Various witnesses gave evidence that, after his conversion, Matt was for a long time paying back to publicans and others the debts that had accumulated during earlier years. Sir Joseph Glynn also made the following statement: "He told a friend that a priest had taught him to love truth and to hate lies."

This evidence, though indicating a true conversion, does not necessarily point to the fact that he had a fixed confessor. But, happily, there is yet extant a tangible link with the seven-year period of Matt's life—his collection of books. Remembering that his early education was meagre and noting his reading in these post-conversion years, it is obvious that he was then, as in later times, under the direction of some zealous and unusually perceptive priest, a priest who was himself a man of prayer.

If the books bearing publication dates later than the year 1890 be set aside, those left form a collection some of which he could have read during the 1884-1891 period; there is, of course, the possibility that of the lot bearing publication dates before 1890, some were bought at a far later date, or lent Matt by friends. But some of the books have leaflets, mortuary cards, etc., bearing dates in the 1880's. It may safely be assumed that they were the books he began with; they are marked in several places. The marked passages, some of which are quoted in the following pages, indicate the trend Matt's spiritual life was taking at this time.

For an almost illiterate man, his first attempts at reading the Scriptures and spiritual books must have meant herculean mental effort. But it also meant that the reader went at snail's pace so all that was read got time to sink in, and to sink deep. Doubtless his heart often failed him and memories of days spent mitching from Brother Ryan's classes for backward boys rose to reproach him; but, having found that in the case of temptation to break his pledge, help to stand firm was there for the asking, he now knew that when difficulties arose in reading, there was also help at hand: "He asked and understanding was given to him."

He told Mr M. McGuirk, a fellow-worker, that he often asked God the Holy Ghost to enlighten him to understand what he read. First among the books he read at this, as at all later periods to his life, were the Scriptures. He had several copies of the whole Bible, besides copies of the New Testamemt and a separate copy of St John's Gospel.

In the Old Testament, the first passage marked is in Deuteronomy, parts of verses 35 and 36:

.... The day of destruction is at hand, and the time makes haste to come. The Lord will judge his people and will have mercy on his servants ...

The next marking is the fiftieth Psalm, the *Miserere*. This Psalm he also had in leaflet form. Both the page in the Bible and the leaflet are much worn. Two other Psalms are marked: the 101st, *Domine, exaudi orationem meam,* and the 142nd. It will be noted that these three Psalms are the 4th, 5th and 7th Penitential Psalms. In the Book of Wisdom the whole of Chapters VIII and IX are marked. Chapter VIII deals with The Further Praises of Wisdom and the Fruits of Wisdom and begins:

She reacheth therefore from end to end mightily and ordereth all things sweetly.

Chapter IX is Solomon's Prayer for Wisdom, beginning with the verse:

God of my fathers, and Lord of mercy, who hast made all things with thy word ...

and continuing

... Give me wisdom that sitteth by they throne, and cast me not off ... that she may be with me and may labour with me, that I may know what is acceptable with thee ... For who among men is he that can know the counsel of God? Or who can think what the will of God is? ... And who shall know thy thought except thou give wisdom, and send thy Holy Spirit from above ....

The concluding two verses marked by Matt in the Old Testament are wisdom IX, 18, 19:

And so the ways of them that are upon the earth may be corrected, and men may learn the things that please thee.

For by wisdom they were healed, whosoever hath pleased thee, O Lord, from the beginning.

Of the various copies of the Bible among Matt's books, two seem to have been more used than others. One was covered with velvet and stitched with clumsy stiches over the original cover; the other was a pocket-sized copy of the New Testament which had evidently been carried about for a long period. The Passion of Our Lord is marked in each of the four Evangelists; in St Mark and St Luke no other passages except the Passion are marked; in St John, II, verses 20-22 are marked:

The Jews then said: Six and forty years was this temple in building; and wilt thou raise it up in three days? But he spoke of the temple of his body. When therefore he was risen from the dead, his disciples remembered that he had said this: and they believed the scriptures and the word that Jesus had said.

St Matthew's was the Gospel most read by Matt

Talbot—possibly because he, too, was a man named Matthew who "rose up and followed."

Chapters V, VI and VII (The Sermon on the Mount) are heavily scored: the Eight Beatitudes; the verses concerning anger and the need for being reconciled to those one has offended; the verses concerning scandal-givers, swearing, and revenge; the injunction to give to those who ask and to those who would borrow; the command to love one's enemies, to pray for those who persecute and calumniate:

> That you may be the children of your Father who is in heaven, who maketh his sun to rise upon the good and bad and raineth upon the just and unjust.

Also marked in these chapters are the exhortations to do the works of justice—fasting, prayers and alms-deeds—not out of ostentation nor to please men, but in secret and solely to please the heavenly Father. The *Pater Noster* is marked; so is the verse:

> Lay not up to yourselves treasures on earth: where the rust and moth consume and where thieves break through and steal.

Also the verse:

> And for raiment why are you solicitous? Consider the lilies of the field, how they grow: they labour not, neither do they spin.

And, finally, the verses:

> Enter ye in at the narrow gate: for wide is the gate and broad is the way that leadeth to destruction: and many there are who go in thereat.
> How narrow is the gate and strait is the way that leadeth to life: and few there are that find it.

In Chapter VIII the reply of the centurian is marked:

> Lord, I am not worthy that thou shouldst enter under my roof: but only say the word and my servant shall be healed.

The only other verse scored in St Matthew, apart from the entire Passion, is Chapter xii, 36:

> But I say unto you that every idle word that men shall speak, they shall render an account of it in the day of judgment.

In Corinthians I, Chapter xiii, verses 4 to 13 are underlined:

> Charity is patient, is kind ... And now there remain faith, hope and charity, these three: but the greatest of these is charity.

Among other books which from dates and cards found in them Matt seems to have been reading at this period, is one well-thumbed volume: *The Principles of a Christian Life,* translated from the Latin of Cardinal Bona. In this book he had marked page 41, The Character of a true Christian; also page 25: The course over which human life runs—its perversity; how our lighter faults and vices are to be corrected; religious persons are more strictly bound than others to perfection.

The former page (25) was marked by a leaflet, which contained an Offering to be made before a picture of the Sacred Heart. The oblation was worded as follows:

> I ... as an act of Thanksgiving, and of Reparation for my many acts of unfaithfulness, give Thee my heart, and I wholly consecrate myself to Thee, my loving Jesus, and by Thy help I propose never more to sin. *(Pater, Ave, Credo).*
>
> Sacred Heart of Jesus, make me ever love Thee more and more.

There was a *Franciscan Manual* dated 1884; in this book the *Good Friday Gospel* is the portion where the pages are most worn; the following extract is written on a blank leaf at the end:

God console thee and make thee a Saint.
To arrive at the perfection of humility four things are necessary:
to despise the world,
to despise no one,
to despise self,
to despise being despised by others.

To Obtain Grace to be Prepared for a Sudden and Unprovided Death is the title of a small torn book.

The Book of Spiritual Instruction, by the Benedictine writer, Blosius, was marked at several points in Section V.

In a very old book by a Jesuit author whose name is not given, *The Practice of Christian and Religious Perfection,* the following points were underscored:

Answer to principal difficulties which usually hinder us from freely discovering ourselves to our superior.

Another answer to aforesaid difficulty.

In what manner we are to render an account of conscience.

Answer to several difficulties resulting from what has been said in preceding chapters.

Of how important it is to receive correction well.

On chastity.

On obedience.

In a booklet entitled *Christmastide* there is a leaflet bearing the aspiration

Lord, Thou has been our refuge always: Live, Jesus!

A Practical Catechism and a very old edition (1770) of *St Augustine's Confessions,* in ten small volumes, may also reasonably be taken as belonging to the books read at this period. The print in these volumes is extremely difficult for anyone to read, and must have been especially so for Matt Talbot; yet four of them are scored on practically every other page.

There is a missal printed by Duffy's, whose publishing house was then on Wellington Quay.

A Life of St Augustine by Moriarty bears signs of having been much used; it is marked at the pages describing St Monica's tears and her death.

Sanctity and Duties of the Monastic State by Dom Armand de Rance, and *Directory for Novices of Every Religious Order* raise the possibility that the question of the religious life was seriously considered by Matt Talbot at this period of his life—between his twenty-eighth and thirty-fifth year.

A book, *The Sinner's Guide,* bears on the fly-leaf, "Dear Mother's book to me after her death," but the writing is not Matt's, and the date, 1871 is more than four decades earlier than the date of Mrs Talbot's death. The following points were marked:

> Of venial sin: Firm resolution never to commit any mortal sin: The effects of Divine Justice (with quotations from Scripture and from the Fathers of the Church on the same): On death-bed repentance: On the death of the just: On the consolations which good men receive from the Holy Ghost: On the Crucifixion: On the Divine perfections.

On the Sufferings of Our Lord Jesus Christ was a translation from the original of a Portugese Augustinian writer, Father Thomas of Jesus.

A History of the Church of Christ, published in Amsterdam, had pages regarding Tertullian marked.

Martyrs of the Coliseum; a very old *Life of St Francis Xavier; Life of St Catherine of Siena*, by her confessor; *Butlers' Lives of the Fathers*, were also in this section of Matt's little library, as was Father Faber's *Spiritual Conferences*, in which the following passages were marked:

> Why so little comes of frequent Confession.
> On death.
> A death precious in the sight of God.
> Confidence the only worship.

In this book the pages were marked by leaflets bearing hymns to St Joseph and to St Patrick. Smaller books included *The Innocence and Penance of St Aloysius, Lives of the Early Christian Martyrs, Lives of the Three Oratorians, Life of St Francis de Sales, Virgin Saints of the Benedictine Order, St Paul and his Missions*, by the Abbé Fouard.

Writings of the Saints included *Leaves from Saint Augustine, Writings of St Alphonsus Liguouri*, with the chapters on death marked; *Our Lord's Words to Saint Gertrude, St Alphonsus Liguori's The Glories of Mary, Treatises on Poverty, and Short Treatises on Prayer*. There was another book on prayer by St Teresa of Avila.

Most, if not all of the books listed above, are those which Matt Talbot read between 1884 and 1891; they took the place of his former drinking companions. They trace the paths taken on the first stage of a long and arduous spiritual journey; the emphasis is on avoidance of sin, acquisition of virtue, consideration of the Four Last

Things, the necessity of constant self denial, mortification and humility for the man whose goal is to be "hidden with Christ in God." "In prayer," runs one marked passage, "man speaks to God; in spiritual reading God speaks to man." These books form our only link with Matt during the seven-year post-conversion period under reveiw.

The following extract, from *The Book of Instruction,* by Blosius, the Benedictine writer, is a typical example of the spiritual reading in which Matt Talbot discerned the voice of God between 1884 and 1891.

Self-denial is both useful and easy to a Man of Goodwill.

1. Self-denial and resignation to the good pleasure of God is the short way to all perfection.

If not earnest, constant and diligent in self-denial and mortification, whatever else a man may do he will make no progress.

... *Unless the grain of wheat falling into the ground die, itself remaineth alone. But if it die, it bringeth forth much fruit* (John xii. 24, 25).

Truest rule of all perfection: be humble, and wherever you find yourself, leave yourseif.

Truest resignation, with profound humility, is the shortest way to God. Genuine and entire mortification is the hiding-place of true and most joyful life.

Excellent exercise—to have a mind always dying to created things; to keep down and humble oneself before every creature.

For he who always dies to himself is always beginning a new life in God.

No more pleasing offering can be made to God than the resignation of our own will, because nothing is more dear to man than his own will and his own freedom.

. . .The servant of God should, frequently, say within

himself: "For Thy sake, O Lord, I desire not to see such a thing, since it is not necessary that I should see it; for Thy sake I will not hear that, or taste that, or say some particular thing, or touch that," He cannot find God perfectly in the secret sanctuary of his soul unless he first puts to death all that is in any way inordinate. Idle gratification of every kind, therefore, must be cut away.

2. When he falls into some defect he should sigh in spirit, not however, with any despondency of mind, even though he fall into that same defect a hundred or even a thousand times in one day. He must call upon God and say: "Alas, my Lord God, see how wicked a sinner am I, in whom vices still live so strongly; I imagined that all self-indulgence was already dead and buried within me, but behold, again I feel a fierce rebellion . . .But I do not despair of Thy mercy. Have mercy on me and help me. For love of Thee I am ready again to leave myself and all things, and behold, I do now leave them." Thus let him pray and then be of good cheer.

3. This constant mortification in the beginning, indeed, is difficult and troublesome. But if anyone will only persevere in it manfully for a time, it will afterwards become by the gift of God truly easy, yea, delightful . . . This art will be learned speedily and thoroughly by him who looks upon all things of this world as no more belonging to him than if his body were already dead, often repeating in his mind the words: *You are dead and your life is hidden with Christ in God* (Col. iii. 13).

During these seven years, while the new Matt Talbot was gradually replacing the old, Dublin and Ireland experienced times not uneventful. Echoes of the excitement of the "Park Murders Trials" in Green Street Courthouse still lingered in the air of the metropolis. The memory of how Kilmainham Prison had been ringed round with ranks of Grenadier Guards, reinforced by infantry and police, while Marwood, the hangman—who was accustomed to hand pressmen his card, inscribed: "William Marwood, Executioner, Horncastle"—executed the Invincibles, was still fresh in the minds of Dubliners.

The winter of 1883-1884 saw the trial in Green Street of four Westmeath men, prosecuted by the Crown for conspiracy to murder a local landlord—resulting in the accidental killing of the landlord's sister-in-law, Mrs Smythe, of Fitzwilliam Place. Edward Carson, the then much-spoken-of "Counsellor" was for the defence; Peter O'Brien, later to be known as "the Packer," was, with The McDermott, the prosecuting Q.C. When the concluding stages of this, one of the most famous legal battles recorded in the English-speaking world of the decade, were reached, Green Street and the approaches to it were thronged by people waiting to hear how "Pether" and the twenty-nine-year-old Carson were doing in the hard-fought battle.

All around the city Carson's speech was being quoted. "Where was the corroboration?" the advocate had asked, "where was the corroborating evidence the Crown was withholding? Where was Hanlon the Informer? The Crown proposed to *read* the evidence of the man whose evidence they had *purchased*. But the informer they dared not produce." Dublin seethed with suspense. He'd get them off. Carson would get them off. But, in the morning, one juror pleaded exemption through fatigue; another protested that a fellow-juryman was "half-mad" and unsuitable for jurorship; a day's adjournment was granted, by which time another juryman had a fit, and, as the Chief Justice would not agree to hear the case with an incomplete jury, there was a postponement till next Assizes. In 1884, at the re-trial, Carson did not appear for the defence, and the jury disagreed. Later in 1884, after a third trial, the prisoners were sentenced to ten years penal servitude each. Peter the Packer, a Sergeant-at-Law, was on the bench when later that year six more Westmeath men were in Green Street and got seven years' penal servitude each for alleged complicity in the same crime—a sentence against which the accused men's vehement protestations of innocence were of no avail.

It was the decade when Parnell had come to the fore; the decade when power see-sawed in England, Salisbury and Gladstone defeating one another by turns in the several elections of the eighties. It was the decade of the new franchise when Irish householders had votes and, in 1885, gave Parnell and his Irish Parliamentary Party 85 out of 105 seats. It was a time when such sights might be seen in Dublin as Father Matthew Ryan, C.C., of Hospital, Co. Limerick, being sent to prison in Kilmainham for refusing to betray his parishioners' affairs to the Bankruptcy Court in a case being fought by the Parnellite Movement. It caused a first-rate sensation in the capital when on March 29th, 1887, Dr Croke, Archbishop of Cashel, the Lord Mayor of Dublin, and a great assembly of citizens, as well as the few faithful Limerick parishioners who had managed to travel to the city for the occasion, formed an orderly procession and marched as far as the jail gates with Father Ryan. A short time previously, the same jail gates had closed on Canon Keller, Parish Priest of Youghal, who was imprisoned for similar reasons; when, on winning their cases in the Appeal Court, first Canon Keller and a few days later Father Matt Ryan were released, they got a great ovation, the crowd that conveyed them to Kilmainham being nothing to that which waited to welcome them on their release.

Cardinal McCabe died suddenly early in 1885. Recording his death, *The Catholic Directory* says:

> His Grace's Archiepiscopacy was cast in troublous times (1878-1885). Distress, awful enough in some districts to be called famine, desolated the land. Agitation, fiercer than any the present generation had witnessed, rose and gathered in its wake. Dr McCabe was an ideal priest, a charitable Christian, a most well-meaning and practical man; but of politics he knew little and about them he cared nothing.
>
> He had striven might and main to bring about some amelioration in the unhappy state of education in Ireland; two days after his death the first slight relaxation of the distinction made by the National Board between religious and lay teachers was made.

In September 1885, Dr Walsh became Archbishop of Dublin. Shortly before that date, one Myles Kelly made public complaint that he was the only Catholic on Rathdown Union Board of Guardians, a body catering for a population more than 75% Catholic. In or about the same time, the *Freeman's Journal* commented on the fact that there was no Catholic on the list of chief clerks of the Irish Post Office, and only two Catholics on the rest of the Post Office staff of higher officials.

Dr Walsh, arriving at Westland Row from Rome, early in September, was met by the Mayor and Corporation, who presented him with an address of welcome. In the course of his reply the new Archbishop said:

For a remedy of the many grievances for the removal of which the people of this island have laboured so long with but partial success, there is but one effectual course—the restoration to Ireland of that right of which we were deprived now nigh a century ago, by means as shameful as any that the records of national infamy can disclose. With you, I rejoice, that the flag which fell from the dying hand of O'Connell has once more been boldly uplifted, and I pray that it may never again be furled, until the right of Ireland is recognised to have her own laws made upon Irish soil, and by the legally and constitutionally chosen representatives of the Irish people . . . Remember, it is to those who seek first the Kingdom of God and His glory that these other things shall be added.

Asking his people for the help of their prayers, Dr Walsh concluded:

Pray that I may ever have the grace to keep in the straight path of duty, never putting forth darkness for light nor light for darkness, never calling evil good nor good evil, and swayed neither to the right nor to the left by the fear of human censure or by the foolish and unprofitable desire of human praise.

Almost the first public duty Dr Walsh was called upon to perform was to bless and open the new Training College for men teachers, St Patrick's, Drumcondra. The year 1885 saw 147 young men, the vanguard of the ceaseless stream of teachers which the Catholic Training Colleges of Drumcondra, De la Salle (Waterford), Baggot Street (later Carysfort) and Limerick, sent out from that time to this. The provision of Catholic teachers for a Catholic country—up to then magnificently served by unselfish, unpaid Brothers and Nuns, their numbers far too few to meet the demands upon their services—made a bulwark, proof against the proselytisers.

Playgrounds for children were being opened in the most crowded areas, the old Liberties; New Row and Pimlico each had one opened, Lord and Lady Aberdeen, the Lord and Lady Lieutenant, being present, as was His Grace, Dr Walsh. The Aberdeens also gave a party for all the old folks of St Patrick's Kilmainham, at the Viceregal Lodge; the Little Sisters' charges spent the 13th of July in the Park, the party ending with songs and dancing—lively headline for Dublin Geriatric Committees of more recent date.

The Papal Envoy, Monsignor Persico, who, with Signor Gualdi, had been sent to visit, inquire into and report upon the actual condition of affairs in Ireland in the summer of 1887 was, in October of that year, invited by the Christian Brothers to the O'Brien Institute where were assembled all pupils, past and present, to greet the Papal Envoy.

One wonders whether, among the thousands of Dublin boys and men who made their way to the O'Brien Institute, a certain past pupil of O'Connell's was to be found. It is possible, that in the initial absorption with spiritual things which followed on his conversion, Matt Talbot knew very little of what went on in the city. His evenings, after work, were spent in some city church. Between 1887 and 1891, no uneventful time in Dublin, there was one citizen, at least, who paid little heed to the history of his Church, his country and his city being made about him.

For Matt the great events of those years were his victories over old habits; the conquest of discouragement, of disadvantages such as lack of education; the poring over a text of scripture, over a paragraph from Blosius; the finding of the key when some bright youngster of his acquaintance, or some workman better educated than himself, pronounced or explained a word that was baffling him; the returning to his reading with the knowledge so carefully garnered and remembered; the earnest prayer to the Holy Spirit; the re-reading of the text, the paragraph—and, suddenly, the understanding dawning, deepening, as the Truth impressed itself like a die on his open, receptive mind. The word "Freedom" was in the air; men were dying for it in the Sudan, in Cuba, in the Philippines, in Japan; men were preparing to die for it in the Transvaal. Had he been asked to define Freedom, it is doubtful that Matt Talbot could have done so. But, in his own spiritual life he was learning "the Truth shall make you free."

CHAPTER VI

IN 1884 MATT LEFT HIS HOME IN NEWCOMEN Avenue, his efforts to induce his brothers to follow in his footsteps having failed. He went to Gloucester Street, nearby, and took a room there. His sister Mary, Mrs Andrews, lived near and did the little cooking he required; she also looked after his room. Her daughter testified at the 1948 Enquiry:

> For a long time after his conversion he was repaying money which he owed for drink. He had had drink on credit and he used to go into public-houses, hand over in an envelope the money which he thought was due, and hastily depart.
>
> My mother told me this story:
> Some time before his conversion, he and his brothers stole a violin from a fiddler and sold it to get money for drink; after his conversion he made a most careful search through all the Poorhouses in Dublin for the man in order to repay the value of what he had stolen; but he was unable to find him.

Several people have told me this story of Matt's search for the fiddler. The late Mr John Robbins, who was very friendly with Matt, told a friend that Matt finally gave the money, with which he wished to compensate the elusive fiddler, for Masses for the latter's soul.

The churches Matt frequented after his conversion were St Francis Xavier's, Gardiner Street; St Joseph's, Berkeley Road; St Saviour's, Dominick Street; St Mary of the Angels, Church Street; the Franciscan Church on Merchant's Quay, popularly known as Adam and Eve's, as it is built on a site adjoining a one-time tavern of that name. Matt's niece gave further details that came to her mind:

Matt was always in good humour; often, in the evenings, I heard him singing hymns in his room. He got on well with others; he was friendly to those in the house, whom he would greet with a cheery word and "God bless you," or "God be with you." His mother told me that he smoked a pipe before his conversion, but after his conversion I never saw him smoking. He was an open and straightforward kind of man whom I could not imagine telling a lie. Matt hated anybody telling lies.

He did hard things—like taking the pledge, giving up smoking, doing severe penances, cheerfully; he was always happy and contented, and you never knew that he was doing these things. He frequently spoke against doing things out of human respect. I heard that he used to take cocoa which my aunt Susan, Mrs Fylan, prepared the night before, and dry bread without butter for his breakfast. He did not eat meat but my aunt told me that for his evening meal she used to boil fish, and Matt used to dip his bread in the water in which the fish had been boiled and he used to give her the fish to bring home with her. My mother used to say: "I don't know in the name of goodness how Matt exists on the small amount of food he eats." We used often to wonder at the same thing. Yet, in spite of the little he ate, he looked well and healthy and he had not an emaciated appearance. In spite of his fasting he was able to do his work.

My grandmother, Matt's mother, told me that he used to get up to pray at 4 a.m. and used to remain up then until it was his time to go out to Mass. My mother used to look after his little room in Gloucester Street and she was the first to discover that he slept on a plank; she used to see a large plank in his room, leaning against the wall at the foot of the bed; she thought he was about to make a door or something of it. One morning Matt apparently forgot to remove it from the bed; . . . . afterwards he left the plank there, and there was no mattress. The frame of the bed was iron, and the plank (which I never saw) was placed on that and covered with a sheet; my aunt, Mrs Fylan, used to wash the bedclothes for him. She told me that he used a block of wood for a pillow. I only heard about the chains he wore when he was dead; Mrs Fylan knew about them when he was alive; she told me about them after his death.

Before I was married, I used to visit him frequently, and I always found him very gentle, good-humoured and ready to enjoy a joke. I never remember him being in a bad temper, though he could be stern. Once, before I was married, I had been out of work for some time and I borrowed ten shillings from my Uncle Matt, promising to repay the money as soon as I got my first month's wages in a new position I had got at the Congested Districts Board, Rutland Square. When I was paid I forgot all about poor Matt. The next time I was paid, a month later, my brave Matt was waiting at the steps when I came out from my place of employment. He called me and said: "Come here, Nanny, didn't I lend you ten shillings and didn't you promise to pay me out of your first month's wages?" I said that I could not pay him then but that I would the next month and he agreed to wait. When I went to pay him at the end of the next month, he took the money and said: "This is what you promised to repay." Then he gave me back the money and said that all he cared about was the principle that a promise should be kept and that a debt should be paid. He used to advise me never to get into debt.

In his room he had no luxuries—only the bare necessaries—a bed, a chair, a table, a crucifix and some holy pictures. His clothes were clean and tidy. I think Mr O'Callaghan* used to give him clothes.

Matt was friendly with Fr O'Callaghan of Berkeley Road; he was friendly, too, with Father James Walsh, S.J., to whom he used to go to Confession. He was always very humble and had a habit of saying "we are all sinners." He could laugh heartily at funny jokes we used to tell him but he himself did not indulge in joking. If ever he had hot words with the men at work he would go afterwards and apologise to them. He would tell you straight out what he thought of you, but he would try not to hurt your feelings. Matt had a great admiration for his parents, and he was very fond of his brothers and sisters, even though the boys were fond of drink. I never heard about the girl asking Matt to marry her until I read about it in Sir Joseph Glynn's book.

The following is the passage referring to the rejected proposal:

It was during this period (1884-1892) that the incident occurred which decided him not to marry. His mother related the story to her daughters. While working on a building job at the residence of a Protestant clergyman, Matt attracted the attention of a cook by his holiness. The cook, who was a pious Catholic girl, seeing that Matt did not speak to the maids as the other men did, decided to speak to him and finally suggested marriage. She informed him that she had considerable savings and was in a position to furnish a home. Matt said that he would let her know his answer after he had done a novena asking for enlightenment. This he did, and at the conclusion of the novena he told the girl that he had got an answer in prayer

* The Mr O'Callaghan referred to here was a Mr Ralph O'Callaghan, owner of Wm and P. Thompson, Wine Merchants, 85 Lower Gardiner Street, who became a great friend of Matt's, but not until about 1912 or 1913.

that he was to remain single. He was very firm in his resolution, as when some of his fellow-workmen in later years spoke of marriage to him he always said he would never marry, as it would interfere with the manner of life he had decided to live. To a confidant he said that "the Blessed Virgin told him not to marry."

There is no clue to the identity of the cook, nor any record of her reaction to Matt's turning down of the proposal. None of the witnesses at the 1948 Enquiry could throw any light on this incident, of which they had not personal knowledge, but a few witnesses at the earlier Enquiry made statements substantially the same as the paragraph just quoted. The fact that Matt made a novena before coming to his decision shows that he thought the idea worthy of serious consideration; it also shows how he acquired the habit of praying about life's problems and decisions; he was in his early thirties, yet he would appear to have achieved a calm far beyond his years—to have succeeded in restoring order and harmony to a hitherto disordered existence. But, while the convert must be admired, one can sympathise with the girl who realised, perhaps before anyone else, that Matt was the best man in Dublin.

To return to the sworn evidence, the testimony of the late Mr Seán T. O'Ceallaigh, President of Ireland, is of interest at this point as it concerns the years between 1890 and 1897. Mr O'Ceallaigh, who was a witness at both Enquiries, stated:

I knew Matt Talbot personally. I came to know him during the time I served Mass at St Joseph's Church, Berkeley Road. I knew him from 1890 to 1897 and I spoke to him occasionally. Sometimes I used to open the door for the 7 a.m. Mass and on such occasions I used to see him waiting at the steps of the Church before the door was opened. Matt got to know two or three of us altar-boys well and used to call us by our Christian names. We used to call him "Mr" Talbot. Sometimes the boys referred to him as "holy Joe" . . . In the mornings he used to wait, kneeling, on the steps of the Church—praying—with his rosary beads in his hand. He usually received Holy Communion at Mass. Sometimes I saw him in church at the evening devotions and I saw him making the Stations of the Cross after these devotions . . . . He used to pray very fervently and seemed to have a great esteem for prayer . . . He prayed for long periods and showed great reverence. Occasionally I heard him pray aloud . . . He had either a prayer book or rosary with him in the church. When he entered the church in the mornings he knelt at the altar rails facing the Blessed Virgin's altar and received Holy Communion there. More than once I saw him pray with outstretched arms; at such times he prayed aloud with his eyes raised to the crucifix and seemed oblivious of everyone. I never saw him sitting in the church; he was always either kneeling or standing. He knelt all during Mass. It was before Our Blessed Lady's altar that he was always to be found; he showed special devotion to her.

He often spoke to myself and some of the other boys. He would ask us if we said the rosary and if we were fond of doing so; he recommended us to say it. He often asked us a question in Catechism and gave us good advice. Sometimes the boys tried to make fun of him, as when they called him "holy Joe." I have never seen him resent the boys' fun at his expense. He was friendly and kind to us. And we were not afraid to approach him; on the contrary, we used to go to him frequently and talk with him. He was **very affable—I remember when I was about ten, Matt** taking me by the hand for a chat and a walk round the church grounds. He was a pleasant, approachable and kindly man. I never saw him angry, he was calm and quiet.

I cannot recollect ever having seen him wear an overcoat. He seemed a poor man; he was poorly dressed; he was neat and clean at Mass. He wore a scarf, then commonly worn by working men instead of a collar and tie. He used to go to Mass in other churches at that time as well as Berkeley Road. I saw him sometimes on weekday mornings at the 6 a.m. Mass in the Dominican Church. On Sundays he heard several Masses. Having seen him at the early Masses in Berkeley Road, when I came back again to serve at 12 o'clock Mass. Matt would be there too. He seemed to be as humble a type of man as one could meet. He certainly did not try to attract any notice. He seemed completely lost to what happened around him when he was praying. I would say that he was the nearest I could imagine to one in ecstasy; his fervour and recollection were extraordinary; he was an outstandingly holy man. he used to kneel all during Mass—upright and without any support; his manner in the church before Holy Communion was most reverent . . . . he would be one of the last to leave the church afterwards. I used to see him making the Stations of the Cross; he would stand and move from Station to Station. I frequently saw him saying the rosary; often he said it aloud when there was no one in the church.

He used to stop and talk to me in the street.

When the President was asked about his statement that Matt Talbot often stopped him and spoke to him in the street, he said that he was referring to the years after 1897, when he ceased to be an acolyte in Berkeley Road Church. Matt used to enquire how he was getting on at school and what grade he was in and how he did at various examinations, usually adding a little word of advice about availing himself of the opportunities schooldays offered; doubtless, he recalled his own mitching! Later still, when the young Seán O'Ceallaigh began to work, Matt, whenever he met him, stopped and enquired how things were and how he was getting on. "We always had a very friendly little chat," Mr O'Ceallaigh said, "and he advised me to mind my work and do it well."

Questioned at the 1948 Enquiry regarding the opinion people had of Matt Talbot during his lifetime and since his death, the President replied that he had not heard many speaking of Matt during his lifetime, but that since his death the fame of his sanctity had spread and was continuing to spread. Matt Talbot's holiness was much spoken of by the general public and a strong desire was also evinced by people of all classes of society for his beatification. The President said that he himself had more than once visited Matt Talbot's grave in Glasnevin cemetery.

When, six years after her brother's death, Mrs Fylan testified she stated that Matt's wages prior to 1913 were 12s. 6d. a week. He used to smoke and chew tobacco before his conversion but shortly after 1884, gave it up. Her sister, Mrs Andrews, giving evidence regarding the post-conversion years, stated:

> Matt was admitted into the Third Order of St Francis on October 18th, 1891. I have his certificate of admission. He took the names "Joseph Francis." I saw him myself doing the Stations of the Cross on his bare knees. I also saw him myself on a couple of occasions outside Gardiner Street Church on his bare knees,* waiting for the doors to be opened in the morning. Others saw him more frequently. His knees were as hard as wood and the side of his head was numb from lying on his wooden pillow. His

---

* Several witnesses, at both the 1931-37 and the 1948-52 Tribunals, testified to the fact that Matt Talbot had slits cut in the knees of his trousers to enable him to bare his knees easily when kneeling.

favourite place in the Jesuit Church was near the altar of the death of St Joseph. He was naturally a bit hot-tempered and sometimes could lose his temper a little but only for a few moments. Almost immediately he would recover control of himself and speak as quietly as usual. If he had, in temper, said anything hurtful, he would go down on his knees and ask your pardon. He was a pleasant man and would laugh and talk with visitors . . . he sought to conceal his prayers and fasts, and he looked for the quietest part of the Church. He would not listen to any praise of himself. He was a very intelligent, sensible man—in no way odd. He was no great scholar but when he spoke of religion he seemed to be very learned. He was strong-minded, determined and plain-spoken.

Sir Joseph Glynn's evidence regarding this period is important; he was careful to point out to the Tribunal that it was based on statements made to him by persons some years dead—Mrs Fylan and Mrs Andrews, and Mr Ralph O'Callaghan, who knew Matt Talbot very well and for a long period. He was referring to the seven years 1884-1891:

He (Matt) kept the pledge faithfully for three months, after which he renewed it for another three months; then he renewed it for twelve months and at the end of that year took the pledge for life. Soon after his conversion he started the habit of rising and praying from 2 a.m. to 4 a.m. each morning.

I was told that soon after his conversion he gave away a new pipe and tobacco to a man who had asked him for a "fill" or tobacco for his pipe. After that he never smoked again.

All the time he suffered intensely from the craving for drink and used to remark to his mother, "I'll never stick it, Mother; I'll drink again when the three months are up." She encouraged him to take it for a further period.

He joined the Sodality of the Immaculate Conception in Gardiner Street Church (Jesuit).

After his conversion he continued to work for the firm of Pemberton's and for the Port and Docks Board. After two or three years he changed over to T. & C. Martin's, the timber merchants, as it was more convenient and enabled him to hear the 6.15 a.m. Mass in Gardiner Street. Work began at Pemberton's about 6 a.m. and at Martin's at 8 a.m.

Regarding the statement that Matt went to work at T. and C. Martin's a few years after his conversion (i.e., about 1887 or so), enquiries among old men who knew him and the firms mentioned, show that it must have been at a much later period he went to work for Martin's on a permanent basis. None of the men who knew him in Martin's could remember him there earlier than 1909, except one, Mr Daniel Manning; and, unfortunately, the firm's records of men employed in the timber yards during the 1890s and early 1900s were not preserved, if such records ever existed. But there is a double record of his having been employed by the Port and Docks Board for a period in 1900.

The Port and Docks Board wages-book shows that he went to work there in a temporary capacity the first week of May 1900. He was one of a group classified as a "Gang". His name appears on the pay-sheets for the following eight weeks—up to July 3rd, for each of which weeks he received wages. For the next three weeks his name remained on the books but he received no wages. After that he was not on the Port and Docks list. The other record of this period of employment with the Port and Docks Board not only confirms the Port and Docks Board entry, but holds an interest of its own. The father of the late Mr G. Holohan, 83 Mobhi Road, Glasnevin, was a foreman employed by the Port and Docks Board. He often spoke of having Matt Talbot working for him. Among Mr Holohan's papers was found one which was evidently a list of men on strike in the Port and Docks Board's Gangs. The headings run as follows:

9-7-1900	Strike Cont.
Out	(Twenty-one names here
(Six names here)	including Matt Talbot's)
"Strike"	
(Fifteen names here)	(Six names here)

Of the forty-two names coming under "Strike" heading, thirty-eight are marked off in pencil, different pencils having been used; this probably indicated that these men returned to work in different batches; four: Dolan, McAuley, O'Reilly and Talbot, were not ticked off and do not appear again on the Port and Docks Board pay-roll. It would seem that Matt, having decided to go on strike, did not change his mind when the strikers' demands were not met; he stayed out. His attitude to strikes, labour conditions, etc., will be referred to in a later chapter; but his stand at this juncture, thirteen years before the big strike of 1913, is worth noting.

It is safe to assume that, like those of his fellows who were not skilled tradesment, he took work where he found it, being taken on and laid off according as the various firms he worked for were busy or otherwise. The strike referred to above was occasioned by the refusal of a demand for increased wages made by the Port and Docks Board employees and the dockers employed by several shipping lines. The *Evening Herald* of July 2nd, 1900, reported that 150 men employed by these concerns struck work on that day, demanding that their wages be raised from 4s. 6d. to 5s. a day and/or from 7d. to 9d. an hour; they also asked for Saturday work to cease at 3 p.m. On July 3rd the same paper said that 500 men were out by that afternoon. The *Evening Herald* of July 9th referred to reports that men were to be brought in from England to take the place of the strikers. Riots developed and the police and strikers came to grips a few times within the next two days; the papers contain long lists of men on strike who were charged with riotous conduct, but Matt Talbot's name does not figure among them.

On the papers of the days preceding July 17th, mention is made of men going back to work in batches, and the final mention of the strike was made in the *Evening Herald* of July 17th, which stated that, as practically all the men were back at work again, the strike might be considered as ended. There was no mention of the workers having got any rise in wages or improvement in working hours. Matt Talbot went on strike. He did not go back to work with the same firm. He probably gave the same consideration and prayer to his decision to strike as he did, some years earlier, to a marriage proposal; if anything, he gave the matter more consideration, as by this time he had doubtless, reached a stage in his spiritual progress when the only thing that mattered in life was to please God.

CHAPTER VII

Books Matt Talbot was reading in the 1891 to 1900 period included a *Manual of Devotion to the Holy Ghost;* a *Life of St Teresa of Avila;* Bishop Hedley's *Our Divine Saviour and Other Discourses;* four volumes of the *Imitation of the Sacred Heart* by Father Arnold, S.J.; *Meditations on the Life of Our Lord,* translated from the French of Father Nouet, S.J.; *Lives of Eminent SS. of the Oriental Deserts; History of the French Clergy During the Revolution,* by the Abbé Barruel. He had a contemporary pamphlet, *David and Goliath: Anti-proselytising dialogue between a hedge-school pupil and Sir Thomas Dross, Souper Knight.* In a worn prayerbook were a series of litanies which he seems to have been in the habit of saying regularly as the feasts came round each year, or daily over a certain period. They included the Litanies of the Holy Name, the Blessed Sacrament, the Sacred Heart, the Litany of the Mercy of God, the Litany of the Infant Mary, the Litany of the Holy Virgin, the Litany of the Undivided Trinity, the Litany of the Ascension of Our Lord, Litanies of St Teresa of Avila, St John the Evangelist, St Ursula, St Angela, St Aloysius, St Rose of Lima, St Francis Regis, St Francis de Sales, St Vincent de Paul, and our own St Dymphna; with these litanies were a selection of prayers and litanies and aspirations for a happy death.

Whenever he read of an Association, the aims or devotions of which attracted him, he evidently sent away his name for enrolment forthwith. In 1892 he sent his name to Baltimore, U.S.A., to be inscribed as a member in the Confraternity of the Agonising. He was also a member of an Association with headquarters in 95 Rue de Sèvres,

Paris, then the principal house of the Vincentian Fathers. In 1894 he enrolled as a member of the Perpetual Lamp Association of Our Lady of Mount Carmel, and had his name inscribed on a card given him in Donnybrook and signed: Fr Bernard, O.D.C. He was enrolled in the Bona Mors Association, Gardiner Street, and had several of the leaflets which that Confraternity issued each year. He joined a Crusade for the Preservation of the Holy Shrines in Palestine; he belonged to the Confraternity of La Salette; in a prayer-book there was a leaflet bearing the address of the Passionist Fathers, Mount Argus, evidently an acknowledgement of a donation sent them, but the name of the sender, the amount sent and the object for which the alms was intended were all erased. Père Grou's *Meditations on the Love of God* contains a leaflet showing that Matt was a member of the Rosary Confraternity. In March, 1899, Matthew Talbot and Charles Talbot joined St Patrick's Roman Legion, an Association under the direction of an Augustinian Father, concerned with raising funds to build a National Church of St Patrick in Rome.

Other books among those of this period were an *Explanation of the Ceremonies of Holy Week; St Catherine of Genoa on Purgatory; The Blessed Sacrament, Centre of Immutable Truth,* by Cardinal Manning; *The Shield of Catholic Faith,* by Tertullian; *Lives of the Irish Saints; Lives of St Bridget of Sweden, St Rita of Cascia, St Gerard Majella, St Catherine of Siena,* another *Life of St Augustine; Our Lord's Revelations to St Gertrude,* and several smaller pamphlets.

The smallest, a tiny booklet about two inches by one and a half, was a reprint of a lecture given by Bishop

Hedley entitled *On Reading*. Matt Talbot evidently read and re-read this booklet. The author listed a few books with which every Catholic should be familiar, Holy Scripture, books on Our Lord, His Blessed Mother and the Saints. A book on the Mass; the *Imitation of Christ;* the *Spiritual Combat;* St Francis de Sales' *Introduction to a Devout Life,* and other works were warmly recommended. Practically every book he listed is to be found in Matt's collection.

In Dr Hedley's little book, Matt Talbot had the following passage marked:

> Even when the newspaper is free from objection, it is easy to lose a good deal of time over it. It may be necessary and convenient to know what is going on in the world. But there can be no need of our observing all the rumours, all the guesses and gossip, all the petty incidents, all the innumerable paragraphs in which the solid news appears half-drowned, like the houses and hedges when the floods are out. This is idle and is absolutely bad for brain and character. There is a kind of attraction towards petty and desultory reading of this kind which is sure to leave its mark on the present generation. The newspapers present not only news, but ideas, reflections, views, inferences and conclusions of every kind.
>
> . . . . As the reader takes in all this prepared and digested matter he is deluded with the notion that he is thinking and exercising his mind. He is doing nothing of the kind. He is putting on another man's clothes, and fitting himself out with another man's ideas. To do this habitually is to live the life of a child; one is amused and occupied, and one is enabled to talk second-hand talk; but that is all. Men were better men, if they thought at all, in the days when there was less to read . . . Immoderate

newspaper reading leads, therefore, to much loss of time, and does no good, either to the mind or to the heart.*

In a Bible with dates and leaflets indicating that Matt used it at this period, 1891-1900, the following were marked: the two opening chapters in Leviticus, the first dealing with holocausts or burnt offerings; the second with offerings of flour, and first-fruits. The words of David to Jonathan in I. Kings xx. 3, were underlined:

There is but one step between me and death.

The twenty-second Psalm, *Dominus Regit Me*, was marked at the lines

He hath converted my soul. He has led me on the paths of justice, for His own name's sake.

The thirty-sixth Psalm, *Noli aemulari*, was also marked, as was the thirty-ninth, *Expectans expectavi*. What sentiments the words must have evoked in the soul of Matt Talbot!

With expectation I have waited for the Lord; and he was attentive to me.

And he heard my prayers and brought me out of the pit of misery and the mire of dregs.

And he set my feet upon a rock and directed my steps.

In the margin beside the forty-first Psalm he wrote: "Beatitude is the Life of God." In this copy of the Bible the forty-sixth Psalm—an invitation to all to praise God—is also marked. The only passage marked in the New Testament is a verse from Luke xiii:

Unless you do penance you shall all likewise perish.

In *Our Divine Saviour and other Discourses*, another work of Bishop Hedley's, Matt marked the concluding

---

* Dr Hedley lived before the advent of radio and television.

lines of a chapter on the Redemption. This was the paragraph marked:

> It is a curious fact that, although there never was a time when men and women were more prodigal of tenderness to created beings, such as wife, or husband, or child, or dependent, yet there never was a time when they put so little of their *heart* into the love of their God. God is hardly a person to them; He is part of a system; He is a far-off First Cause. The world will not remember that *the Word was made flesh, and dwelt among us, and we saw His glory.* The proudest, richest, cleverest man among us all has nothing left him, when he realises that, but to kneel down and be a little child. *I thank Thee, O Father, Lord of Heaven and Earth, because Thou has hidden these things from the wise and prudent, and revealed them to little ones. Yea, Father, for so it hath seemed good in Thy sight.* To kneel at the crib, to kiss the crucifix, to follow the Stations of the Passion, to weep for the sufferings of Jesus; it is not the wise and prudent that know the wisdom and the prudence of this.

A chapter on the Real Presence is marked at a commentary on St Luke's expression, "their eyes *were held* that they should not know Jesus," in the Gospel narrative of the two disciples who went to Emmaus on the first Easter Sunday.

The book most heavily marked of those read at this time is the four-volume *Imitation of the Sacred Heart,* by Father Arnold, S.J. In Book I the passages marked are all concerned with the forgiveness of sin, the longest one dealing with the firm reliance the soul should have upon the power and readiness of Our Lord to forgive sins. Book II has passages marked dealing with the need for faith in Christ's Divinity, and showing how the Sacred Heart teaches us to live the life of faith. A heavily scored two lines reads: *The Sacred Heart living in the world teaches us how to dwell in the world that we be neither of it nor harmed by it.* Book III is marked at the section "On Compassion for Jesus Suffering," and Book IV at a page where souls are warned against desiring visions or revelations. Further pages marked in this work are the "Love of the Most Sacred Heart as manifested in the wonderful Sacrament of the Blessed Eucharist," "That we must prove ourselves before approaching this holy Sacrament," "On the Love of Solitude," "Asking for the Gift of Prayer."

In a Meditation on Death and Judgement, wherein occurred the passage marked in the Bible (I. Kings xx. 3): *There is but one step between me and death,* that line was again marked, and another from Tertullian: *There is no to-morrow for a Christian.* On a card was the text: *Blessed are they who hear the Word of God and keep it.* There was a saying from St Augustine: *To penitents I say: To what purpose is it that you be humbled if with this you be not changed.* Another marked passage reads: "Reflect daily for five minutes on death and the nothingness of all that passes with time. Act in all things like one convinced that nothing is truly great but what is eternal." And again: "If sinners do not punish themselves in time, the Divine Justice will punish them in eternity. If the Holy of Holies fasted, prayed and wept, what should not be done by such vile wretches as we are."

In Father Faber's *Spiritual Conferences,* the chapters on Death were marked, particularly the chapter, *A Death Precious in the Sight of God*—perhaps one of the most moving and devotional chapters in all Father Faber's writings. Also marked was the chapter, *Confidence the Only Worship,* and the chapter headed *Why so little comes of Frequent Confession,* which the famous

Oratorian and convert based on the axiom: Holiness depends less upon what we do, than upon why and how we do it; here, too, Father Faber listed several of the ways in which self-love can sap and undermine the purity of intention, can deflect the soul from looking steadfastly, simply and exclusively to God in this sacrament of His Mercy. The other volume of Father Faber which Matt had, *All for Jesus,* he later on gave to his friend, Mr John O'Callaghan, Richmond Road. Matt had written on the fly-leaf.

> Three things I cannot escape:
> The eye of God
> The voice of conscience
> The Stroke of Death.

and elsewhere the following:

> In company guard your tongue
> In your family guard your temper
> When alone guard your thoughts.

In St Francis de Sales' *Introduction to a Devout Life* he has marked: Chapter XIV (Part II) "Of the Most Holy Mass and How We Ought to Hear it"; Chapters IV, V and VI (Part V) "Examination of the State of Our Soul towards God; In Regard to Ourselves; In Regard to Our Neighbours." He had also a small book, a collection of maxims, and several leaflets with printed quotations from the works of the Saint-Bishop of Geneva.

A little book, on *Silence and Recollection,* by Dr Murray, Archbishop of Dublin (who died in 1853) was also in this period's books; another bore the title *Spiritual Consoler for Christians of Timid Conscience.* There was a book of Instructions by Dr Hay, and a work by Tertullian, *The Shield of Catholic Truth.* Matt seemed rather interested in Tertullian. In another work, a *History of the*

Church of Christ, the pages with reference to Tertullian are all marked.

But there was some reading apart from the strictly spiritual; this included *History of the Roman Empire*, *History of Peter the Great of Russia*, and a volume entitled *Leo X and the Character of Lucretia Borgia*. The latter work was possibly acquired by the Servant of God to supply himself with sufficient knowledge to argue with someone who—ignoring St Francis Borgia—was judging the Church by the standards of the other Borgias. A rather suprising item in the collection was a small book entitled *University Life in the Middle Ages*, as was a book of this period, Newman's *Loss and Gain*, evidently often perused. Brother Ryan's "mitcher" had certainly come a long way—mentally as well as spiritually! In connection with Newman, three of whose works Matt had, the following testimony was given at both Enquiries by Mr Daniel Manning, who worked with Matt in Martin's:

> On one occasion (i.e. while working at Martin's) during the last decades of Matt's life, I saw him reading Newman's *Apologia pro Vita Sua*. I remarked that it was a very difficult book to read—that I had tried to read it myself and found it very hard to understand. He said that when he got hold of a book like that he always prayed to Our Blessed Lady, and he believed that she always inspired him to take the correct meaning from the words.

Another employee of Messrs T. & C. Martin in Matt's time there was Mr Edward Carew of Dargle Road, Drumcondra. In the course of his evidence, Mr Carew stated:

> I remember on one occasion he told me that he was reading the book of Deuteronomy. I laughed at the idea, and asked him how he could understand such a book. He

told me that he prayed to the Holy Ghost and so would understand it. He did not speak in any spirit of ostentation. I believe he had many religious books but I never saw them. On one occasion he borrowed a history from me, which he later returned.

Another witness, Mr Edward (Ted) Fuller, Great Charles Street, confirmed Mr Carew's statement.

And Mr Michael McGuirk, Middle Third, Killester, who like the preceding witnesses quoted, worked in T. & C. Martin's adds:

Matt used to read pious books; he used to lend them to the other men. He used to tell stories of the lives of the Saints, which he had probably read; and he used to send men to the bookstalls to buy books.

At the 1931 Enquiry, Mr John Gunning, giving evidence regarding his friend Matt Talbot (with whom he became acquainted about 1895) stated:

....He lent me the *Life of St Catherine of Siena* ... I introduced him into the Contraternity of the Living Rosary at the Dominican Church of St Saviour's ....I asked him if he had read in the *Life of St Catherine* that she wore a chain. He looked confused and said he supposed she did ...One day he told me that he had read of a devotion which lifted him from earth to heaven. I asked him what it was and he said it was wearing a chain. This devotion, he said, made him a slave of Our Blessed Lady ...Some time after that I asked him to get me a chain. He bought one and brought me to Clonliffe College to Dr Hickey. Dr Hickey was out and we saw Fr Waters* ...Matt got Fr Waters to enrol me as a slave of Our Lady, too, and I wore the chain ...†

---

 * Afterwards Monsignor Waters.

 † This devotion was strongly recommended by St Grignon de Montfort in his spiritual classic, *True Devotion to Mary*, a book Matt Talbot possessed.

Rev. Brother Furlong S.J., Sacristan at St Francis Xavier's Church, Upper Gardiner Street, Dublin, who knew Matt well from seeing him in the Jesuit Church, testified as follows:

> He asked me once did I read the lives of the Saints and specially mentioned, I think, St Catherine of Siena. He said, "They are wonderful."

The nineties and the early years of the new century would seem to mark the second stage of Matt Talbot's spiritual progress—if his reading be a true indication of the paths he pursued. What a change has come over the man who, before 1884, was leading a drunken, careless and, according to himself, sinful life! He has turned over a new leaf; he has steadily persevered in avoiding sin and is trying to keep close to God. Where before there was disorder and agitation, now all is order and peace. He keeps climbing steadily, reaching new heights of virtue to discover other ranges still higher and, in the far distance, the sublime, seemingly unscalable peaks of holiness, bathed in a light too bright for human eyes to gaze upon undazzled. With the realisation that God loves him springs up a desire for God, and thirsting for the everlasting fountains, he looks for one who knows the topography of the spiritual Everest. Having found a guide, he follows his directions. Matt Talbot's director, having assured himself of his penitent's sincerity, generosity and humility, evidently indicated and supervised the reading on which the soul of this workman was to grow so strong and travel so far.

"The power of thinking," says Father Faber, "which a system of education engenders in those subjected to it, is the best test of that system: the second test by which an educational system is to be judged is its successful creation of a taste for reading." Matt Talbot, in his youth, had had no education worth speaking of; but since his twenty-eighth year he worked to make up the leeway, solely for God's sake and with no thought of self-interest. First of all he had to struggle with the mechanical difficulties of reading; no small task, as any teacher who has helped others to master the extraordinary phonetic divergences of the English language can tell. Reading, especially the slow laboured reading of Matt's post-conversion years, resulted in a steady accumulation of vast stores of knowledge of spiritual matters.

To the man who had never been taught how to think, his reading suggested lines of reasoning, helped him to come to conclusions; he gained time by gleaning in his books the experience—especially the spiritual experience—of others. "It is instructive to observe," says Father Faber again, "that when God is pleased to raise ignorant and illiterate persons to a high state of perfection, he infuses into them supernatural science, making them very frequently even accomplished theologians and profound expositors of Scripture; as if knowledge must lie in the spiritual soul either as a cause or an effect of holiness, or more probably as both."

This constant reading about God, Our Blessed Lady, the angels and saints, the soul and the virtues, was to Matt Talbot a continuous source of inspiration. Had he not, in one of the books of the 1884-1891 years, marked the words: *In prayer we speak to God, in spiritual reading and sermons God speaks to us.* His reading—to which he gave several hours daily—was, for him, what the earlier spiritual writers so well called it, "oil for the lamps of prayer". By degrees, his mind became peopled with thoughts of God and holy things. Placed as he was, with neither rule nor superior, in no cloister, but toiling ceaselessly in the midst of the hard world, he needed to keep his mind, the citadel of the Spirit of God, occupied with thoughts that would act as a strong and loyal garrison in surprise attacks by the triple enemy columns—the world, the flesh and the devil; he had to know how to deal summarily with the traitor self, so strongly entrenched, so cunningly disguised, in Everyman.

His reading saved him from building spiritual castles-in-the-air; it cast out listlessness. It made his personality more attractive—this taste for reading—as under its gradual influence he expanded. The men who worked with him came to realise that, by some means—some lever unknown to them—he was raising himself, infusing an element of greatness into all he did. He had an inner serenity which others recognised in him, while feeling that they themselves lacked it. And the more he read, the more illuminated his mind became, so much the more his spiritual horizons widened. He was able to appreciate that there are different ways for different men, that God "fulfils Himself in many ways."

Above all, Matt's achievement in acquiring and fostering and developing this taste for the spiritual, freed him from human respect; he lived so constantly in the presence of God and of the great and holy minds his reading put him in contact with, that the judgements of this world lost for him the magnified importance men usually attach to the opinion of their fellows.

Though Matt Talbot obeyed to the letter St Paul's injunction, "Mind the things that are above," he could hardly have been unaware of the happenings in Dublin towards the close of the 19th and at the beginning of the

20th century. Ireland—too long a province—should be, said her patriots, "a nation once again." The eighties had seen the rise of Parnell, the nineties, his fall. At the turn of the century, Arthur Griffith had published the first number of *The United Irishman* and, early in the new century, John Redmond was elected Chairman of the re-united Irish Parliamentary Party. The celebration of the centenary of the '98 rebellion had caused to glow again the long-smouldering, unquenchable embers of partiotism. The Boer War, which started in 1899, showed the authorities that there was a good deal of pro-Boer sentiment in Dublin, as elsewhere. On the very streets being decorated for the Queen's visit in early 1900, ballad singers were drawing the crowds with "Kruger Abu!" (sung to the air of O'Donnell Abu!) or with that other popular refrain:

> The Boers, they were marching
> And the British wanted fight
> The Boers took out their long-Tom
> And blew them out of sight
> Sound the bugle! Sound the drum!
> Give three cheers for Kruger
> To————with the Queen and her ould Tambourine
> And hurrah for Kruger's Army.

"Queen Victoria," wrote John J. Horgan in *Parnell to Pearce*, "then eighty-one years of age, as a mark of her appreciation of her Irish soldiers, abandoned her annual visit to the South of France and came to Dublin instead. She stayed for three weeks and was, on the whole, well received, driving unescorted through the streets . . . Some people. with a mixture of incredulity and malice not uncommon amongst us, went so far as to allege that the old lady did not actually realise where she was and believed herself to be in France. I saw her one afternoon,

113

during her visit, outside the Mater Misericordiae Hospital, Dublin, while she listened to an address of welcome, her heavy Hanoverian face rising large and somnolent over the side of the carriage."

Young Mr Horgan—a Corkman—was a pro-Boer himself, as were many of his fellow-students attending the lectures prescribed by the Incorporated Law Society for solicitors-to-be. Oliver St John Gogarty, W. B. Yeats, Tom Kettle, Eoin MacNeill, Father Eugene O'Growney, were all names well known to the students. In 1893, Dr Hyde, Father O'Growney and Eoin MacNeill founded the Gaelic League. Father O'Growney spent the last six years of his short life writing text books and phrase-books. Dr Hyde was, by 1900, crossing swords with the formidable Dr Mahaffy and his Trinity colleague who had belittled Gaelic as a "peasant *patois.*" In the Gaelic Theatre an Irish play, *Casadh an tSugáin,* was a rather startling innovation. The beautiful Miss Maud Gonne was known to be practising her part—a daring patriotic part—in a play, *The Countess Cathleen,* by W. B. Yeats. Arthur Griffith, a Dublin journalist, just back from South Africa, was knee deep in MSS, printers' ink, blocks and all the rest of the paraphernalia of newspaper production in the little Liffeyside office where the *The United Irishman* was struggling to come out weekly and keep clear of debt.

Many were reading the novels of Canon Sheehan, the Parish Priest of Doneraile, Co. Cork. David P. Moran was writing trenchant articles in *The Leader,* tackling such vested interests as the brewing industry, the music-hall stage, and the railways. Madame Nellie Melba, whose singing captivated Dublin in 1893, was back in 1900. Even in the seven year interval between Madam Melba's two visits, life in the capital had changed somewhat.

114

In May 1896 the first electric tram travelled from Haddington Road to Dalkey. As everyone had expected to be electrocuted by the current from the overhead lines, there were many sighs of relief when the run was accomplished without casualty. January 1910 saw the last of the 186 horse-trams—cream for Donnybrook, green for Harold's Cross, purple for Palmerston and brown for the Pheonix Park—that had served the city for so many decades previously. The older people sighed and wondered what had become of the 1,000 horses—ordinary drawing-horses and tip-horses for the gradients too steep for the two-horse teams—and the big bay, Tullamore Hero, the tip-horse at Portobello Bridge, a horse known to the whole city. No good would come of the new fangled craze for speed, the elders remarked, recalling the tram-and-ship collision at Ringsend in the 1880s.

Willie Jameson's horse, "Come Away," won the 1893 Grand National—on three legs and at four to one. The Earl of Fingall's "Cloister" won the following year's. Sir Horace Plunkett drove the first motor-car Ireland had seen, up and down the Park, and occasionally down Sackville Street. Mr Winston Churchill, fresh from his journalistic experiences in the Boer War, came and lectured in Dublin, but he forgot to mention the Irish regiments and his speech fell flat. In the silence after the speaker had resumed his seat, the following speaker, Justice Fitzgibbon, tried to make up for the omission. The Cadogans and Dudleys and Londonderrys and Wyndhams and Balfours came and went between the Castle and the Park, between London and Dublin, and wherever they went their satellites followed.

For 1894 the British Board of Trade Returns listed fifty-one Irish Trades Unions; for 1895, ninety-three. At the early Trades Union Congresses the agenda dealt largely with grievances such as night work in bakeries, sweated labour, non-Union labour being employed by firms engaged on large government contracts, and the habit of employing boys to do men's work. In 1896, a twenty-six-year-old Ulsterman, hardly known in Ireland, though he had been for some years active in the Scottish labour movement, was being spoken of in Dublin labour circles; his name was James Connolly and he founded the Irish Socialist Republican Party. Early in the new century, Connolly emigrated to America.

Occasionally, Dublin workers were visited by another Northerner, James Larkin, a man of magnetic personality and great driving force, whose own terrible experiences as an exploited youth in Liverpool and elsewhere, gave him authority to speak—and to get a hearing. Jim Larkin's first visits to Dublin were to organise the unskilled workers. There was a rather sharp cleavage between the skilled and unskilled workers in the capital; the former were organised in their Unions and considered themselves a class apart from the "unskilled" exploited workers; the dockers, carters and casual labourers were victimised by tenement landlords, money-lenders, publicans and others. The Gaelic League, Sinn Fein, movements for Industrial Revival such as Horace Plunkett's, meant little to this host of unorganised workers who—their attention perpetually concentrated on the grim struggle for existence— had neither the time nor the heart of engage in any movements for their own betterment. It was this "Submerged tenth" of the Labour world that Jim Larkin aimed at organising.

Matt Talbot belonged, in so far as he was an

"unskilled" worker, to this class; but, being unmarried and having reduced his wants to a minimum through the ascetic life he had voluntarily chosen, he did not himself perhaps feel hardships as others did; and, if he did, his reaction to discomfort would probably be different from that of others. That is not to say that he was insensible to the miseries of his fellows; it will be shown that not only was he keenly alive to the sufferings of his acquaintances, but in his own way did what lay in his power to help those whom the misery of their times and circumstances hurt most.

CHAPTER VIII

IN MARCH, 1899, MATT'S FATHER, CHARLES Talbot, died and Matt went back to live with his mother at 23 Middle Gardiner Street. The sisters, all but one who married late in life, were married. Charlie had a shoe-shine stand, sometimes outside Amiens Street Station, sometimes outside the General Post Office. John, the steady fellow, was in a position of trust with the Port and Docks Board. Bob had died in 1886, aged twenty-eight. There is no account of those hard drinkers Joe and "The Man" Phil, at this period; perhaps one or both of them volunteered during the Boer War—in which case their brother, Matt, would have been likely to say a few words when they came home on furlough, pointing out that Irishmen were famous for fighting for every country but their own. Among his books were not a few cuttings and pamphlets, as far back as that period, showing where his sympathies lay. Early in the century he got permanent employment with T. & C. Martin's, a firm for whom he had worked fairly regularly—when not working for the Port and Docks Board, or Pemberton's—in the previous decade.

T. & C. Martin Ltd, a firm which originally traded under the name of John Martin and Sons, could trace its origins as far back as 1798, the year of the ill-fated Rebellion. In 1855, on the retirement of an elder member of the firm, the name was changed to T.& C. Martin's, T. and C. being the initials of the founder's grandsons. At the same time a separate firm was started by Richard Martin, another grandson, on the south bank of the Liffey, with offices at the old Mercantile School buildings. In 1886, T. & C. Martin's became a private limited company; subsequently, Richard Martin's also became a limited company. Later, both concerns were to amalgamate.

Matt Talbot was glad to change to Martin's; work did not begin there as early as in the Port and Docks Board, so he had more time for Mass. Daily Communion then, even for religious, was rather unusual; among Matt's books for this period was one on the practice of weekly Communion. To go oftener would certainly have drawn attention in those days. The following extracts give some idea of his daily routine and the conditions under which he worked. Matt's niece, Mrs Johnson, told the 1948 Tribunal:

> My mother and aunt told me that Matt fasted and did penance to make reparation to God for his sins of drunkenness. He spent his time at work or at prayer. He spent his free time either at home or in the church. He did unusual penances, but at the same time they were not excessive and he was able to do his work; I never remember his being ill, only two years before he died, when he took ill, with heart trouble, and was in hospital for some time.
>
> I heard that he knelt on the steps outside Gardiner Street Church before the door was opened for Mass. The Mass in Gardiner Street was at a very early hour. After Mass he used to come home and have a cup of cocoa, after which he went to work which began about 8 a.m.

A memorandum issued near the end of last century by the Port and Docks Board, through their Manager to the Head Foreman, gives an insight into the rates of pay, working hours, etc., and the normal conditions obtaining at the time.

2 Septr. 1899.

On and after Monday next and throughout the year, the breakfast hour in the Custom House Docks will be from eight to nine o'clock.

On and after Wednesday next the rate to be paid for overtime to *all labourers* will be sixpence per hour.

On and after Wednesday next the rate to be paid to men working at deals all day (that is to say men who commence work at six a.m. and finish at closing time) will be 4s. per day exclusive of overtime. The man in charge of the work will keep a daily way-bill of the men working under him which is to be returned to me on the following day.

(Manager's signature).

There was at this time, a dispute between the Port and Docks Board and the employees, mainly owing to an objection by the permanent workers to a concession whereby the casual workers got the same rates for overtime. A perusal of the correspondence and newspaper reports of this dispute shows that working hours in the docks were 6 a.m. to 4 p.m. Three-quarters of an hour was allowed for breakfast and half an hour for dinner. One letter from the Manager to the Board asked that the breakfast-time be extended to one hour "as in other places"; other points from this letter were:

... It is the almost invariable practice in every bonded warehouse to allow only half-an-hour for dinner. I may say, however, that when our men are employed at heavy labour discharging ships, they are always allowed one hour for dinner. The rate of wages paid varies according to circumstances. Ordinary labourers are paid 18s. per week; gangers and storemen, who are drawn from this class, receive more, and boy labourers less. I consider that 18s per week, regularly earned, not to speak of overtime, is very fair remuneration for the work performed. Railway porters and wine porters do not, as a rule, receive as much ... No complaints have ever been made by the men themselves officially of either rate of pay. In fact I am at all times overwhelmed with applications for employment at these rates; members of the Dockers' Union, who receive casual labourers' pay of 4s. 6d. a day prefer to come to us at 18s. a week, a certain 18s. being preferable to the uncertaintly of casual labour at a higher rate. Besides which our men receive a pension, medical attention and sick relief money.

Matt Talbot had been employed at the Custom House Docks Section for eight weeks before the dispute. In a letter written some months earlier to the Port and Docks Board by the Docks Manager, reference was made to wages elsewhere, including T. & C. Martin's.

The Distillers Company only pay 16s. to 17s. for similar work; their men attend at 8 a.m. with breakfasts eaten, get half-an-hour for dinner, and have to work until 7 or 8 p.m. if required, without overtime, and get no pensions. Messrs T. & C. Martin, who handle more deals than any firm in the Port, pay their men 18s. per week for ordinary timber work, and 6d. per day extra for piling deals.*

Mr Joe Nolan, a retired employee of T. & C. Martin's, said he remembered Matt Talbot very well; he was hard-working, and it often struck Mr Nolan that carrying the timbers either to the stacks or to be creosoted must have been very hard on Matt, "for he had the most sloping shoulders of any man I ever saw; and he was a very small man, too. You would wonder how he could keep the deals on his shoulder, with such a slope."

---

*These figures are higher than the 12s. 6d. a week which Mrs Fylan (Matt's sister) said her brother earned weekly up to 1913 (cf. p. 96).

Edward Fuller, another fellow employee, gave the following evidence at the Apostolic Process:

> I knew Matt was very severe on himself, praying much and going out to early Mass—I used often to see him passing my door on his way to the 6 a.m. Mass in Gardiner Street Church. He used to pass about 5.45 a.m.

> His sister told me that he used be up about 4.30 or 5 a.m. When I knew him he worked as a labourer in T. & C. Martin's; at one time he was in Creosote Boilers (creosoting timber)—very hard work; later he worked in the saw-mill, carrying deal timber to the mills from the timber-piles; later again he assisted Mr Harry Kearney in the hardwood drying shed; later again he was in the part of the yard known as Castle Forbes. He was honest and hard-working and an excellent timekeeper. He never wasted his employer's time; if he sometimes was found praying it was at times when he was waiting for something to do—he availed himself of this time for praying. Mr Gethin, Manager of the Mills, who used to give Matt his orders, told me that he (Matt) was a good, honest workman who never neglected his duty. Mr Gethin had great trust in Matt to do anything. At his mid-day meal he took only tea or cocoa and one little piece of bread.

Perhaps the people who knew Matt Talbot best during his working-hours were the Manning family, who lived from 1904 to 1926 in a house in the portion of T. & C. Martin's yards known as Castle Forbes. Mr Daniel Manning said, in the course of his evidence, that when he first knew Matt Talbot, the latter was engaged in loading timber; later he remembered him working in Castle Forbes yard.

> He was a most conscientious workman, who would not waste a moment of his time. When he had time free, e.g., during lunch hour, I several times saw him reading or praying. My belief is that he had his own method of

122

praying and did not merely recite prayers which he had off by heart. It was common knowledge that he went to daily Mass (6 o'clock) in Gardiner Street after which he might take something to eat and then went to the 7 a.m. Mass in St Laurence O'Toole's Church—on his way to work. Sometimes I think he received Holy Communion in the Church of St Laurence O'Toole and had a light meal prepared for him by Mrs Manning (wife of witness) before beginning work.

He used to make a visit to the Blessed Sacrament in the same church on his way home from work. He was very abstemious with regard to food. My wife told me that at his mid-day meal she used to make at his request a mixture of tea and cocoa. She remonstrated with him and he said he was doing that as a "little penance."

In spite of his penance he was able to do his work. He took particular care of doing what he was told to do regarding his work. He was a good, conscientious workman. He tried to avoid notice; he carefully avoided all ostentation, especially as regards his penances. He was a very silent man; he was retiring, with no interest in worldly things; but he would answer politely when spoken to. He went about with his eyes cast down.

Once I asked him had he seen some item of news on the placards; he replied that he never looked at the placards, that he was not interested in such matters. ...I never met anybody like him. He was totally wrapt up in God. He was always in good humour, yet he led a holy life perseveringly; he was very popular with his fellow-workers, who respected him as a holy man.

He was very punctual; he used to open the yard, presumably by arrangement with Mr Carew, and was always there before the hour. He was very nice and obliging always.

Matt spent some time every evening after work in St

Francis Xavier's Church. I think it was he himself told me this.

His work was more or less routine; he never made difficulties about doing it; he was always anxious to do his work, even extra work if occasion arose. He was always mild and agreeable and gentle. He was not a storeman in the yard, just an ordinary worker; he would be handed written orders from Head Office for sale or distribution of timber; his job was to see that the timber was loaded according to order. If any special difficulty arose he might have to refer to Mr Carew. He impressed me as a man of calm, even temperament, though inclined to get a bit fussy at times—if people were rushing him with work. But generally he was quiet and genial, good humoured and easy to get on with. He could not say anything harsh under any circumstances, though I can easily believe that in his earlier life he may have had a struggle with himself to overcome his strong temperament.

If the reminiscences of old Pat Doyle, as given in the earlier chapters, be recalled, it will be seen how far Matt had advanced from the days when the Talbot men were forever wrangling and roaring and "having arguments."

Mrs Manning, in her evidence, supplied some details that a womam might be expected to notice:

I do not think he ever bought new clothes. In the morning, coming to work, he wore a long tail-coat—"swallow-tail"—and a hard bowler hat. When he came to the yard, he took off his good coat and put on working clothes. I think he wore clothes some friends gave him and never bought a suit. I never saw him wear an overcoat. He was always very clean and tidy in his dress. In between loading the cars, my children often saw him on his knees praying in a little shed in the yard. Sometimes they saw him there praying with arms outstretched; he was not praying aloud.

When finished his work in the evenings he always washed his face and hands with cold water at a pipe in the yard. He did not dry his face and hands and would not accept the use of a towel I offered him. Then he took off his old clothes and a sack he used to wear over his shoulders carrying the timber, and put on his good coat and hat and went to St Laurence O'Toole's Church. I saw him going there and Canon Flood, now dead, told me Matt used to visit there in the evenings. He always told me which Saint's Feast it was; his normal conversation was about the feast of the day; his only interest was heavenly things. He seemed to have studied the lives of the Saints and he had particular devotion to St Teresa of Avila and he used to call St Therese of Lisieux a "wonderful little girl." He was specially fond of one of my children—Teresa—whom he used to bring by the hand around the yard, sometimes teaching her her prayers, sometimes speaking to her about her patroness, St Teresa, telling her to imitate her.

The men usually left the yards at 5.30 p.m., but Matt left at 5 p.m. because he worked during the lunch interval—or portion of it. One evening I was in the house about 6 p.m.; the yard had been closed and everyone, as I thought, had gone home. There was a knock at the back door of my house which led on to the yard. I was rather frightened, wondering who it could be—and it was dark. I asked who it was and Matt replied. He said he had been "saying a few prayers" and did not notice the dark coming on; the yard door being locked he had come to ask me to let him out through the house.

For his midday meal he took a mixture of tea and cocoa—a small amount—in a billy-can; he allowed it to get cold and took it without milk or sugar. I never saw him eat but I heard he ate only dry bread. The can from which he took this meal was covered with sediment at the bottom. One day I asked him if I might wash it for him, but he said "No"—to leave it as it was; he said he liked it that way "for a little penance." He was always very cheerful and good-humoured.

I regarded him as a holy man, as did the men who worked with him—and so did Father John Flood. I cannot think of any particular reason why I thought of him as holy—there was something about the man which I cannot explain. To all outward appearances he was just an ordinary workman. The other men restrained themselves in his presence. They respected him and did not regard him as being in any way odd or peculiar. When he spoke about the saints I listened to him with respect and reverence. He was the most extraordinary man I ever met; he impelled respect. Father Flood, then senior curate at St Laurence O'Toole's, respected him highly; when he died Father Flood went to his funeral in Glasnevin. Matt was always happy; he was cheerful and good-humoured. I could not imagine him angry.

One of my daughters told me that on one occasion when they and a child, Annie Markey—who later died a very holy death—were playing in the yard, Annie carelessly said, "O God!" Matt rebuked her and said that she could not come to play in the yard again unless she promised not to call the name of God in vain. On a later occasion she did come back, and Matt heard her take God's name again and expelled her from the yard. I was sorry for the child; I remember at the time asking my daughters what had happened and they told me as I have related. I heard that he used to reprimand the men in the yard if they used bad language.

He always kept his eyes cast down walking along the street. On one occasion I met him in the street and saluted him but he did not answer. Afterwards I told him that I had met him and that he had not returned my salutation. He replied that he always kept his eyes on the ground and had not seen me.

Granby Lane, Dublin, showing the spot where Matt Talbot died.

Photography: Richard Dann

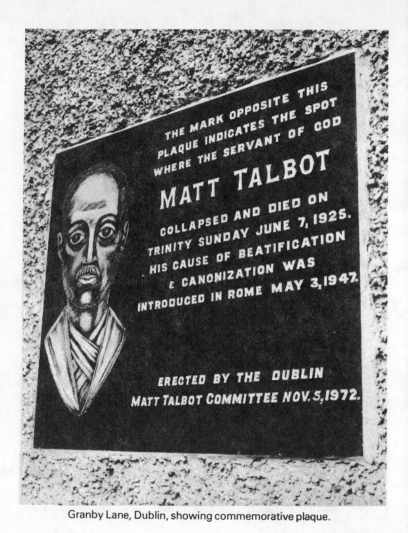

THE MARK OPPOSITE THIS
PLAQUE INDICATES THE SPOT
WHERE THE SERVANT OF GOD
MATT TALBOT
COLLAPSED AND DIED ON
TRINITY SUNDAY JUNE 7, 1925.
HIS CAUSE OF BEATIFICATION
& CANONIZATION WAS
INTRODUCED IN ROME MAY 3, 1947.

ERECTED BY THE DUBLIN
MATT TALBOT COMMITTEE NOV. 5, 1972.

Granby Lane, Dublin, showing commemorative plaque.

Photography: Richard Dann

MATTHEW TALBOT
1856-1925
SERVANT OF GOD

Matt Talbot's tomb, church of Our Lady of Lourdes,
Sean McDermott Street, Dublin.

Photography: Richard Dann

Liberty Hall, Dublin

Photograph: Courtesy Independent Newspapers

Once he found some eggs my hen had laid in the yard and came to me with them. I said that he should not have bothered bringing them but should have kept them for himself. He replied "No—they were not mine to keep."

On another occasion, when he was speaking to me, Mr Martin, Manager of Martin's, came along. I did not like to be seen by Mr Martin talking to Matt, as he might have concluded that I was wasting Matt's time, and I was going to move away when Matt told me to stay where I was. "You need fear no man," he said, "there is only one Person to remember," and he pointed towards Heaven. He was very fond of my children, but from his conversation with them and with me—all about God and His saints—it is clear that he was anxious that myself and my children should please God and so earn Heaven.

Giving further evidence regarding Matt's day in the timber-yards, Mr Fuller testified:

Between the time when the timber had to be loaded, I often noticed Matt Talbot kneeling in prayer in the hard-wood drying shed. In wet or cold weather he knelt with a sack over his shoulders. When I called him he used to say: "All right, I'll be there in a moment."

Interviewed on the same subject, Mr Fuller remarked that in the early days of his acquaintance with Matt, he often called him and it would be some minutes before he replied. Then he (Mr Fuller) discovered that Matt did not seem to like to be found praying, so from then on his friend adopted the expedient of knocking a board, or shouting to someone else, or coughing, to let Matt know he was coming; this ruse was successful. Mr Fuller would hear Matt rising from his knees and usually met him coming towards him.

According to Mr Fuller, Matt, on his way home from work and after visiting St Laurence O'Toole's made a second visit to the Blessed Sacrament in St Joseph's, Portland Row. Sometimes Mr Fuller went in there with him and saw him kneel prostrate, and kiss the floor before going to a quiet place at the side of the chapel. Mr Fuller usually stayed about ten minutes, but always left Matt behind him there. He mentions that Matt always spoke of Our Blessed Lady as the "Blessed Mother of God." He often said, "Praise be to God," or "Thanks be to God." If he heard others abuse the Holy Name, he would respectfully and silently raise his hat as a gesture of respect and reparation.

Mr Fuller's evidence throws some light on the Talbot family.

> When his two brothers (Joe and Charlie) died, there was no money to bury them, as they had spent it all on drink. Matt did not like the way they had spent their lives; when they died, however, it was he who paid their funeral expenses. Bob died in 1886, only two years after Matt's conversion. He was then twenty-eight. Charlie, ' the shoe-shine merchant, died at the age of thirty-four—in 1908; (he had been the youngest of Elizabeth Talbot's big family).

> Matt wore (Mr Fuller's evidence continues) the same clothes on Sundays as going to work; they were too big for him and had the appearance of being clothes that he got from somebody else. I called to his room one evening; there was not much furniture—a small bed and a stool, some small holy pictures, a crucifix and a holy-water font. I do not remember whether there was a table or not; though his clothes were poor he was clean, tidy and modest. He never wasted time; any free time he had he gave to prayer. He was naturally of a quiet disposition, though he could be roused for a moment if things went wrong. He would then walk away in silence and

"cool down"; he would use harsh words on such occasions but never fail to ask pardon. On various occasions I heard him admit that he was wrong—in regard to some item of work or in the ordinary course of conversation. At such times he would say: "You were right, and I was wrong." When he discovered that he was in the wrong he never made excuses for himself.

Several of his fellow-workers testified to a habit Matt had of keeping a pebble in his mouth—a small, smooth pebble which he carried about with him. No one asked him why, nor did he volunteer any explanation. Mr O'Callaghan of Richmond Road relates that his friend, the late Mr John Robbins, was a particular friend of Matt's; they used to lend one another books, and Mr Robbins was one of the few people who visited Matt in his room in Rutland Street, where he lived alone for the last ten years of his life. When Mr Robbins called, Matt would ask him to take out his pipe and light up; the visitor did not like doing this as he thought it not quite right to enjoy in the other's company a comfort of which Matt was depriving himself. But Matt would insist; "I have this," he would say, going to the mantle piece and fetching a pebble; "now, light up, John, and enjoy your smoke." Then there would follow a discussion of the last book read, while John Robbins puffed away at his pipe and Matt sucked meditatively on his pebble.

Sir Joseph Glynn has listed the extraordinary fasts Matt undertook. These were in adition to his life pledge from alcohol and his strict observance of the then severe Church laws concerning fast and abstinence during Lent and Advent, and on Ember Days and certain vigils.

During Lent a complete black-fast (no-milk) every day on two slight meals without meat or butter. During June, in honour of the Sacred Heart, a similar black-fast. Every Wednesday, no meat, but occasionally a little butter. Probably the full Franciscan fasts after their abrogation by Pope Leo XIII. At other times of the year his routine was: Sunday, his ordinary dinner at 2 p.m., that being his first meal of the day; if this were fairly substantial he did not eat again, but if it were a light meal, he partook of cocoa or tea and bread again about six o'clock. Monday, dry bread and black tea; Tuesday—if not a vigil of a feast or a Lenten Tuesday—breakfast consisted of cocoa and bread and butter, dinner of a little meat; Thursday was as Tuesday, Friday, a full fast. As he got older he found the dry bread hard to swallow; to enable him to eat it without butter, he got his sister to boil a whiting and steeped his bread in the water in which it had been cooked; he did not eat the fish which he gave his sister to bring home. But when his health broke down in his late sixties and he had to abstain from work, he ate whatever was recommended and would take meat, an egg or bread and butter.

He concealed these fasts from outsiders by making it a rule never to refuse food if pressed to have a meal. Besides this severe régime, begun some years before 1899, if not at the actual time of his conversion, he slept but four hours nightly, later not even so long; the little repose he allowed poor "Brother Ass" was taken on a wooden plank, with a timber block for a pillow, and with scanty bed-covering. The continuous denial of food and sleep was not the sum total of the intensely penitential life this quiet workman was leading. He wore chains. There is little need to mention the chains, for it was the finding of these instruments of penance on Matt Talbot's body after his death that showed not only the immediate world in which he lived and worked, but also the late 19th and early 20th century in which his days were passed, that there had been an unknown one in its midst "of whom the world was not worthy."

Few of the witnesses before the Tribunal who had worked with him, had any idea that he practised such constant and severe penance. Perhaps his own people wondered less at his penances than those outside Ireland.

The spiritual heritage of the Irish, handed down through the centuries, has certain characteristics that distinguish holiness in Ireland from holiness in other lands. The footprints of the man who first sows the good seed of the Gospel remain in the field of his apostolate, as the soil where he sows—the racial temperament—retains certain native characteristics. Thus, in the way of holiness, there comes up again and again in Ireland, Patrick's mystic union with God that overflowed constantly in prayer and labour, in mortification and zeal; there is still in the people to whom Patrick preached, a generosity, a vehemence and an instinct for devotion akin to that found by the Apostle in their forebears.

Throughout the centuries the seal of St Patrick has stamped itself on the piety of the Irish; today, as fifteen centuries ago, certain racial traits are manifest in Irish Catholicism. In the men who went forth during the first great missionary era—it is called the first, for in the 19th and 20th centuries the world witnessed Ireland's second missionary age—from Columba in the Scottish isles in the North to Columbanus crossing from the Jura to the Vosges, to the Alps, to the Appenines—in them all there was something of Patrick; yet they were all Irish of the Irish. The most penitential pilgrimage of Medieval Europe was, with its stress on inaccessibility and austerity, a challenge to every Christian worthy of the name. Shane Leslie has described it in his book, *Saint Patrick's Purgatory*. The pilgrim began by making his confession; then he fasted for a full fortnight on bread and water. For the next five days Office for the Dead was chanted morning and evening. Finally the penitent was placed in the centre of the church under a pall and a Requiem Mass was offered for him. Though the modern pilgrimage to Lough Derg is not as rigorous as it then was, still it is probably the most penitential pilgrimage left in a world where pilgrims' travel is made not only easy but pleasant, and where their exercises at the pilgrimage centres, though still devotional, retain little of austerity.

Later on, in the lyrics of *Tadgh Gaedhaelach* and other poets of Ireland's silenced Church, the same austere tone was mingled with the intensely devotional. In the holy lives that have lit up the decades before and since Matt Talbot's time—Father Henry Young, Edel Quinn, John McGuinness, Father John Sullivan—the same traits are found. Perhaps the most pronounced characteristic to be discerned in Matt Talbot's piety was his asceticism. His spirit of mortification and penance have been misunderstood, not only by those who recognise no value in self-denial save as a means of developing willpower—subduing of the lower to the intellectual self—but also by many who associate asceticism with inhibitions, glumness and other modern miseries.

"Asceticism" derives from the Greek verb *askein*, meaning to exercise; it is the putting into spiritual practice of the ordinary principles dictated by prudence and by the experience of others who have aimed at and achieved a goal. St Paul's words to the Corinthians, indicating the example of their athletes, who denied themselves—"they for an earthly crown; we to gain one that is everlasting"—were penned by the Apostle when he was explaining that the mainspring of true Christian asceticism was the motive which prompted it. The body is brought into subjection, neither for its own sake, as in the case of the athlete, nor for the sake of developing will-power, not yet for the sake of conquering the lower nature that the intellect might benefit by the energy diverted to and canalised in it. Mortification has always been regarded by the Church not as an end in itself, but as a means to an end, the end being the love of God; the malice of sin being chiefly in the rebellion of the will—"I will not serve"—so the true value of penance is in the will, faithfully endeavouring to conform itself in small things as in great, to the Will of God.

Matt Talbot, seeking to serve Christ, translated, into the terms of his own life, the text *If any man love me let him deny himself, take up his cross and follow me.* Holiness is nothing if not diverse in its manifestations; all ages, all nationalities, all classes have known it—yet it is rare, so rare that when men come across it some wonder, and some are scandalised. Like his friends, the Saints, whose lives he loved to read and in whose company he had come to feel at home, Matt was so convinced of God—the Creator, the End of Man—that he lived with an intensity and at an elevation far beyond that of his fellow-men. In his seeking to be like Christ he found that certain things entangled his spirit, so he freed himself from them. He once told a friend that the hardest time of his life was the first few months after he took the pledge, when the craving for drink returned again and again pleading for appeasement. The first steps were the hardest; after that it was only a matter of a step at a time. He had copied

David's words: "There is only a step between me and death." Nothing mattered but to keep on—walking towards God; walking in the footsteps of Christ.

The old man, Pat Doyle, who knew Matt Talbot in his youth, said emphatically: "Matt only wanted the one thing—drink." Mr John Monaghan, Clerk of St Francis Xavier's Church, who knew Matt well in his later years, when asked about him, said: "He would reply if you greeted him, but you had the impression that he would rather no one spoke to him. Matt only wanted the one thing—God." That his penances scandalise some is not strange in times devoted to the cult of comfort and bodily ease; to see a poor uneducated labourer making strides along the road all Christians know they should try to follow—even if only by keeping to the less thorny margins—is for some an incentive, for others a reproach. To Matt Talbot, intent upon God, his penances were a very literal fulfilling of Christ's command, *Deny thyself . . . follow me*. They were but a means to an end.

CHAPTER IX

THE EVIDENCE GIVEN AT BOTH ENQUIRIES indicates that Matt Talbot was receiving spiritual direction continuously, from the time of his conversion until his death. This fact is rather important as it has a bearing on the insinuations made that the Servant of God was simply following his own bent in regard to the life he led, that his mortifications were but aberrations, and that the man himself was either an exhibitionist or a poor creature wavering on the border-line between sanity and insanity.

The first priest mentioned was Dr Keane, who gave Matt the pledge at Clonliffe College in 1884; later that year Dr Keane became a Dominican. That Matt remembered and was grateful to this priest is evident from the number of cuttings he kept, notices of sermons preached by Dr Keane in Dominick Street or other city churches.

Edward Fuller gave evidence that Matt went to Confession once a week:

> He told me that he used to go to Confession every week at Clonliffe College; he went regularly every Saturday to his confessor, Dr Hickey; I think he used to have talks with this priest and it was Dr Hickey who recommended him to read the Lives of the Saints. Matt told me that he and this priest were great friends.

Mr Edward Carew corroborated this:

> I often heard Matt speak of Rev. Dr Hickey, for whom he had great respect.

Rev. Brother Furlong, S.J., stated:

Mrs Halbert, who knew Matt very well, told me that he was intimate with Rev. Dr Hickey. She also said that she heard that he was friendly with a Father O'Reilly of the Pro-Cathedral, Marlborough Street.

Mrs Johnston said:

Matt was friendly with Father O'Callaghan, Berkeley Road, and with Father James Walsh, S.J., to whom he used to go to Confession.

Mr Wm Larkin also gave evidence on this point:

I saw Matt going to Confession sometimes to Father Walsh, S.J., in Gardiner Street.

The late Mr John Robbins of Mountjoy Square, who was a witness at the first Enquiry had this to say:

I knew Matt Talbot for about thirty years or more before he died. I met him daily at work and I used to visit him in his home at Rutland Street; but not often, because I felt that I was interrupting his devotions and that he would have to make up for the time he spent with me, though he assured me I was always welcome. I fully agree with the popular opinion that he was a man of extraordinary sanctity. He made what I considered a heroic sacrifice in giving up smoking, for he had been a very heavy smoker, using seven ounces of tobacco in the week. When he decided to give it up he went to his confessor in Clonliffe to take a pledge against it …Matt once told me that on one occasion when he went to Confession to a Dominican Father in St Saviour's, the priest drew the slide, looked at Matt without saying anything and closed the slide again. Matt did not explain what he thought of this, but my interpretation was that God had enlightened that priest as to the state of Matt's soul …

Sir Joseph Glynn, in his *Life of Matt Talbot*, related that Father James Walsh, S.J., knew Matt very well, and that not only was Matt in the habit of going frequently to Clonliffe to Dr Hickey to Confession, but Dr Hickey was in the habit of visiting him in his room at 18 Upper Rutland Street. Sir Joseph tells that a few weeks before Doctor (then Monsignor) Hickey's sudden death in January 1925 (some months before Matt's own sudden death) he was visiting a parishioner in St Mary's, Haddington Road, to which parish he had been appointed a short time previously, when the talk turned on answers to prayer; Monsignor Hickey said that when he wanted a very particular favour he always got a poor old man, named Matt Talbot, to pray for it and that his prayers had never been refused.

Interviewed in 1953, a priest who was a sudent in Clonliffe in the early years of this century, remembered quite well how Dr Hickey sometimes told the students that there was a very holy man whom he often went to visit. In fact, the seminarians, getting to know that Dr Hickey thought "the world and all" of this old man, would ask him time after time—though the answers were always the same:

"Where were you all the evening, Doctor?"
"Up with the holy man I was telling you of."
"And what do you do when you visit him?"
"We sing hymns a little, and we chat together. He's a holy man."

As the evidence is fairly strong that, for a very long period, Matt went regularly to Dr Hickey for Confession and spiritual direction, the question at once arises as to what sort of man Dr Hickey himself was. The priest who directed such an out-of-the-ordinary penitent, must have been an extraordinarily enlightened confessor. In a memoir of Dr Hickey, the late Dr Myles Ronan wrote:

It is difficult to sum up Dr Hickey's personality. He was the nearest approach to Pope St Pius X that I have ever met in my fifty-four years of priestly life—and I knew both men well. He was a very saintly man. He was the most popular confessor imaginable—none of the students wanted anyone else. He was my own confessor for three years and his gentleness, kindness, understanding and advice were beyond anything I ever experienced in my time at Clonliffe; he inspired the College with a new spirit.

He was one of the two Chaplains from Clonliffe to Mountjoy Prison and was constantly receiving visits from prisoners just discharged after serving a term, or from others whom he had befriended on their release. Before they returned home they were all, of course, hard-up for money and clothes; but he never let them go without emptying his pockets. Often he must have seen through their stories and stratagems, and he could not but know that their visits were made with the object of getting help; his kindness made little of that. He had a great big heart.

He had not much of a voice, but he used to sing at clerical dinners and gatherings. He had one very popular ditty that he picked up in Rome when a young student at Propaganda College; it was a little Italian song poking fun at the Capuchin Fathers: *Padre Capuccino, siete un birbo* (Capuchin Father, you are a rogue!). It was his rendering of this that used to give such enjoyment to his listeners. He just sang it without any attempt at humour or interpretation—like those little lads we hear on Radio Eireann in that popular "The School Round the Corner" feature. No matter how often we heard it, his simple manner made it always sound fresh. He had been eight years at Propaganda and spoke Italian perfectly.

His acts of charity were innumerable; one in particular I

remember. There was a certain citizen of Dublin who had become a chronic alcoholic. Dr Hickey knew that the then Archbishop, Dr X——, was sorry to hear of the sad state to which this man had come, and he (Dr Hickey) went after the poor fellow, visited him every other day, looked after him and was friend, companion and adviser to him until the end, when he was there to support him in his last moments.

This pen-picture of Dr Michael Hickey shows him to have been a priest of more than ordinary discernment, holiness and wisdom. Besides being a man of considerable intellectual attainments and great personal charm, he seems to have retained right through life an unspoiled innocence and a sense of wonder which neither time, nor the contacts he made with men—some saintly, some sin-soiled, some cynical—lessened, much less marred.

The Church, though it requires Catholics to confess their sins at least once a year, does not oblige anyone to seek spiritual direction. Those who put themselves under direction do so voluntarily and because they hope thereby to gain some spiritual advantage. "No man," it is said, "is a judge in his own case," least of all in the case of his own spiritual state. Those in earnest about their souls think it wiser to ask someone else to counsel them in the uncertainties, opportunities and decisions that present themselves, lest God be defrauded by that self-interest which is always ready to slip counterfeit weight into its side of the scales. By spiritual direction is meant, strictly speaking, the steady instruction and encouragement of individual souls striving for perfection. For such direction there must be, obviously, the person who needs and seeks guidance and the individual—almost always a priest—who is consulted. But not so obvious, because invisible is a third: He Who prompted the first to ask for direction and Who aids the director to be a good guide. A modern spiritual writer says: "At the head of all and above all directors is the Holy Spirit."

In the matter of direction, as in that of mortification, Matt Talbot saw not an end, but a means to an end. In St Francis de Sales' *Introduction to the Devout Life,* a chapter of which is entitled "The necessity of a Guide to conduct us on the Way of Devotion," he read examples from Scripture and the Lives of the Saints, showing how God provided guides for those who sought and prayed for guidance; he read of the humble and earnest dispositions needful in the penitent, and of the confidence he should place in his Father in God: "Have the greatest confidence in Him, mingled with a holy reverence, yet so that the reverence diminish not your confidence, nor your confidence hinder in any way your reverence." Francis de Sales, himself a wonderful director of souls, says that to be fitted for his office, a director "mut be full of charity, of knowledge, and of prudence." In Dr Hickey, Matt found just such a Father and friend.

It is quite possible, and it is certainly in keeping with what his friends tell of Dr Hickey, that the latter helped Matt in his earlier difficulties with the printed word. Apart altogether from the spiritual content of the books read by the Servant of God, it will be noted that, according as he advanced in years, he became capable of reading and appreciating books that made ever greater and greater demands on his memory and intelligence as on his ability to reason and to arrive at conclusions. As events in Ireland in the first quarter of the 20th century—the last twenty-five years of Matt Talbot's life—were to have a tremendous bearing on the citizens of this country, particularly those of Dublin, it is interesting to note the turn Matt's reading took after the turn of the century.

This quiet workman, intent only on God and the things of God, suddenly finding himself drawn with his fellows into the vortex of industrial dispute, realised that he had now to equip himself for an active apostolate. As a citizen of a country fighting for its freedom, he had to enquire first what steps a Catholic might rightfully take with regard to securing freedom; having ascertained what was right and what was wrong, he took his stand. The following chapter will show this change in him. For the present, it is sufficient to mention that from 1900 on, Matt Talbot would seem to have referred any practical difficulties he encountered to his director, for his later reading gave the Catholic answers to the problems of the times.

Though his reading had improved since his few-and-far-between schooldays, the same cannot be said of the remainder of the "three r's." He always wrote a poor hand, his spelling was weird, and his arithmetic had to be propped with Ready Reckoners, and table-books and laboured home-made tables. On one piece of paper he had carefully calculated twenty times the numbers 19, 20, 21, 22, 23, 24; thirty times the same set of numbers and forty times 16, 17 and 18. This paper he used for a marker in a small copy of the Scriptures he evidently carried in his pocket; it was also a help to him in calculations he made when the timber was being stacked or loaded.

Mr Fuller, in an interview, told that at one period Matt got moved to a more responsible job in the timber yard which involved some calculations; previous to that he had been for a long period at the arduous work of carrying the timber to the creosoting apparatus and thrusting the planks into the steaming tar-vats. Matt was pleased with the change; "It wasn't such a dirty job," Mr Fuller explained, "and Matt was a very clean and tidy little man; he liked to be spotless. I think it was on account of going to visit the Blessed Sacrament after his work. Not that he ever objected to doing other work; but he used to spend a long time washing himself and taking off any tar spots he might get on his clothes before going on to the Church. He did that out of respect for Our Blessed Lord in the tabernacle; he had a wonderful idea of the cleanliness, even of body, that was becoming to those approaching the Blessed Sacrament. He took a foot-bath every night before going to Holy Communion; he always was poorly dressed but he was never untidy and, as for cleanliness he was as particular as a gentleman born.

But I was speaking of the change of work; this new job meant that he had to make some calculations; I don't know that it meant any rise in pay—if it did it only meant more for Matt to give away in charity—but he was pleased about it and he came to me and said, 'Ted, I don't know will I be able for this.' And I replied, 'And why not, Matt? Isn't it much lighter than the work you have been at all along? And you're not as young as you were.' 'It's not that, Ted,' he said, 'but I'm afraid I won't be able to make up the loads'; he wasn't much good at calculating numbers. I said, 'I'll come round to-night, Matt, and show you,' and so I did and told him that if he was in difficulties I would be working nearby and all he had to do was to give me a shout. He got on all right; once or twice he called to me and I helped him out; he was never very good at figures."

On other scraps of paper similar calculations were made; the papers were used for book-markers, thus serving the double purpose of being at hand when required and of keeping the place when next he could snatch a moment to listen to God. A few notes made by Matt on the margins of various books may be of interest:

The yc zcar czar* of Russia his income is 20 mill year his demain is big as Ireland.

Denis Lacy shot dead 1922 Glen aherlow.

MacCulagh's hour is from 3 to 5.

Mr Mc Cugh's hour is from 2 to 3 to 5 and 7 to 8†

Charles Talbot, 23 Middle Gardiner Street 16th March 1899 (date of father's death).

Laurence Murray Doyle, R.I.P. April 1899 for 2 years.

In the lifetime of Philip Neri there were 15 Popes.

Robert Staples, R.I.P.

Manresa Press, Roehampton.

In 1832 Gardiner Street Church was opened. Father Curtis was made Rector of the Jesuits in Gardiner Street in 1843.

The following are some of the writings relating to God and the spiritual life found in Matt's handwriting:

God is the wisdom of a purified soul.

My God, my great God, my Life, my Love, my Glory.

Who can understand sins? From my secret ones, cleanse me, O Lord: (14) And from those of others spare thy servant.

God will not ask us how eloquently we have spoken but how well we have lived.

Ps. XVIII. V. 13: Cleanse me, O God, from unknown sins .... Deliver O Lord.

---

* Reproduced exactly as in entry. The word "czar" obviously presented difficulties.

† This and the preceding entry seem to indicate that Matt enrolled friends willing to make a Holy Hour at set times.

But that man would make use of God for his own glory is beyond what we can think of.

To know God and to understand His ways and to watch in His presence in all sanctity is the great end of life.

God is the wisdom of purified souls. Man can fly from everything in nature but he cannot fly from himself.

As to nobility of blood, true nobility is to be derived only from the blood of the Son of God.

God, says Saint Augustine, can only be honoured by love.

The obedience of Jesus Christ to the will of God was the recognition of the Sovereignty of God over the will of men.

I ask you O God to blot out my sins in the Name of Our Lord Jesus Christ.

Jesus Christ is at once the beginning, the way and the immortal end which we must strive to gain, but above all in Holy Communion He is the Life of our souls.

Let us not forget that Jesus wished to be cursed on the Cross that we might be blessed in the Kingdom of His Father.

As I cannot receive Thee, my Jesus, in Holy Communion, come spiritually into my heart and make it Thine forever.

The Son of God by becoming man sanctified all the states and conditions of men. Jesus was not always preaching nor healing but he always prayed and suffered.

O Most Sweet Jesus mortify within me all that is bad—make it die. Put to death in me all that is vicious and unruly. Kill whatever displeases Thee, mortify within me all that is my own. Give me true humility, true patience and true charity. Grant me the perfect control of my tongue, my ... (unfinished).

How I long that Thou mayest be master of my heart my Lord Jesus.

Jesus, says Origen, is the Sun of Justice arising with the Spring of Grace upon our hearts.

The Heart of Jesus is with me. Stop, cease. The inhabitants of Antioch, it is related, once arrested a violent earthquake by writing on doors of their houses, Jesus Christ is with us, Cease.

1. Draw me after Thee, O Heart of Jesus, and I shall run in the odour of thy ointments.
2. Grant me, O Jesus, Thy Grace and love and I shall be rich enough.
3. The sparrow hath found herself a house and the turtle dove a nest to deposit her young. Thy heart, oh Jesus, shall be my nest and repose.
4. May my eyes and my heart be always on the wound of Thy Blessed Heart, O Jesus.
5. Who shall separate us from the Heart of Jesus?
6. Heart of Jesus, be Thou the object of all the affections of my heart.
7. Lord, give me of that water flowing from Thy Heart and I shall never thirst.
8. Heart of Jesus support the weak, clothe me with Thy strength.

Mary, Mother of Jesus, pray for me.

O Mary conceived without stain, pray for me who fly to thee. Refuge of sinners, mother of those who are in their agony, leave us not in the hour of our death.

O Blessed Mother obtain from Jesus a share of His folly. Oh Virgin I only ask three things—the grace of God, the Presence of God, the Benediction of God.

The Blessed Virgin Mary is glorified by our devotion to the Angels.

The Angels merit our love for they will assist us at the hour of death.

The Angels help us in Temporal things.

St Teresa and angels—(nothing further written here).

St Teresa was once weeping. She was asked why she wept, and she said for three things—GOD—SOUL—DEATH.

Let us heed what St Bernard says: Who shall give water to my eyes now and fountains of tears to my head that I may prevent weeping in hell by weeping now?

St John speaks of the lust of the flesh, the lust of the eyes and the pride of life. They are nothing else but the love of pleasures, the love of riches and the love of honour *(St John ii, 16)*.

St Ambrose says that without combat there is no victory and without victory there is no crown.

Francis Xavier was born 1506.

What think ye of Christ? (This was written on the back of a picture of Christ teaching in the Temple).

The remainder of the *scripta* dealt either with the spiritual life or with Catholic doctrine or devotion. The following examples give a fair idea of the whole:

The spiritual life consists in two things—mortification and the love of God.

Poverty is the foundation of Christian perfection—make this den of thieves a house of prayer.

True devotion to the Blessed Virgin—Grignon de Montfort. (This note was evidently a reminder to buy this well-known book; it is in the Servant of God's collection).

Faith is an act of the will. It cannot be forced on men.

There are 72 churches to the honour of the Blessed Virgin within the walls of Rome.

There were twenty-one German translation of the Bible—15 in high German, 6 in low German before Luther, and Luther himself used a translation of St Nicholas of Myra which appeared in 1473.

Obedience to the lawful authority is of right Divine.

It is a fact that spirits act upon matter.

The word transgression denotes a criminal opposition to authority.

When you go to Confession you ask the Priest for his blessing: the Priest says, "May the Lord be in your heart and on your lips that you may truly and humbly confess your sins."

Virtue is one of the most excellent things in Heaven or on earth, and so few follow it.

It is not our bodily presence that makes us belong to the world, but an attachment, an affection for its miserable vanities.

Man can fly from everything in nature but he cannot fly from himself.

Conscience means the knowledge which each man has of his own acts.

The human soul is a barren soul in which useless and noxious herbs constantly spring up. IX (9) We must practise being holy and do penance always.

The Kingdom of Heaven was promised not to the sensible and the educated but to such as have the spirit of little children.

The exterior acts of religion are three—Adoration, Sacrifice and vows.

Three substances were united in Christ—His Divinity, His Soul and Body.

Man enjoys by the Union of God to his nature an advantage which the angels never possessed.

One *Our Father*, one *Hail Mary* in honour of the life of ignominy of Jesus, offer yourself to God with joy and peace.

What do I want to speak to you when I have Jesus to speak to me?

There are many other longer extracts, but the above suffice to show how carefully Matt read, noting down what struck him; some of the answers suggested that he had asked to have certain ideas explained, or defined—perhaps by his confessor—and later jotted down the answer. These writings were found, some on the scraps of paper in his books, others on papers found in his pockets, others on the margins of books; there was also one paper bearing a prayer for his spiritual director; this, unlike the others, was not in his own handwriting.

But Matt himself wrote the rough draft of a letter to a priest in Birmingham, ordering some medals. "I want 3 medals sent to 18 Upper Rutland Street to Matt Talbot, Dublin."

And one wonders what led to the inclusion of such an extract as:

> Sir Henry Wotton, a great authority on the point, Ambassador at Venice, tells us that an Ambassador is one sent to foreign Courts to invent lies for his country's good.

While this life of intense, but hidden, spiritual activity was being lived by Matt Talbot, movements in Ireland were gathering momentum, for the Big Strike of 1913 was looming ahead, and beyond that the Rising of 1916.

Before the strike Mr Raphael O'Callaghan became acquainted with Matt Talbot. In his evidence at the 1913 Enquiry, he stated:

> I came to know him first about 1912 or 1913 through an aunt of mine in one of whose houses he lodged. Previously I had heard from her of the remarkable life he led, of his spirit of prayer and love of spiritual reading ... of the Masses he heard. Furthermore, Matt's mother had shown my aunt, privately, the plank bed on which he slept. I felt much interested in this man whose life was so devout and penitential. My aunt suggested that I lend him some of my spiritual books and give him some of my clothes as he was very poor at that time. In this way he came to my house at Windsor Road, Palmerston Park, and from that till his serious illness in 1923 he came fairly regularly at least three or four times a year for books or clothes ... When he first came to my home he was somewhat shy but

subsequently he seemed to be quite at home with me and usually had a chat; on two or three occasions he accepted some slight hospitality ...

I deliberately drew him out and enjoyed his visits. At our first meeting I tried to ascertain whether he was quite a normal man—free from eccentricities and with commonsense views on religious matters. He made a most favourable impression on me; when leaving I lent him the three large volumes on Christian Perfection by Rodriguez. As I said, he called afterwards at regular intervals to receive or return books; he was most particular about returning them. Occasionally he lent me books, one being *The School of Christ*, by Père Grou, S.J. He seemed to be greatly attracted towards spiritual reading and was well acquainted with religious subjects generally, including the lives of many Saints. He could converse freely and with confidence on such subjects. St Catherine of Siena, St Teresa of Avila, and St Magdalen de Pazzi were Saints for whom he used to profess special admiration, referring to them on one occasion as "grand girls." Amongst other books I lent him was *True Devotion to Mary*, by Blessed Grignon de Montfort.

In manner he was very plain, but natural and unaffected. He was direct and outspoken in his speech. If interested or moved by his subject he became at times quite animated, occasionally almost vehement, using gestures to give emphasis to what he said ... Though practically uneducated, he read books by such writers as Faber and Manning with great pleasure. He impressed me as being shrewd and clear-headed and possessing a strong will. There was nothing whatever nervy or over-wrought in his manner or anything to suggest that he was in any way unbalanced. To converse with him even for a short time was sufficient to be convinced that he was a man altogether and unreservedly given to religion. His faith, devotion and sincerity were apparent in all he said on religious subjects; one never felt that there was anything "put-on."

... He freely admitted his habits of intemperance in his youth and would say, "I was terribly fond of drink," and tell how God had given him the grace to give it up and what a struggle it had been for him to do so. Apart from this it was not his custom to speak deprecatingly of himself. He told me that he fasted during each June in honour of the Sacred Heart, but he never mentioned to me any of his other mortifications or alms-givings or his vigils of prayer. I was surprised to read of them in Sir Joseph Glynn's *Life of Matt Talbot*. When he told me of the June fasts I was surprised, and it seemed to me that he should not have spoken of them to me, but I now think that he may have done so to encourage me to follow his example. His speech was blunt straight-forward, and transparently honest but uneducated and unpolished. His accent was that of the ordinary person of Dublin's poorest districts. He often said to me that God had given him the gift of prayer, but made this statement without any self-complacency; I am quite sure that he really did humbly attribute this gift to God and spoke of it only out of gratitude to God. He was a manly type to whom a certain sort of self-deprecatory speech would be repugnant.

He seemed to be altogether given to God and loved to speak of Him and seemed to want to speak of nothing else. In Drane's *Life of St Catherine of Siena* which I lent him he read of how God addressed the Saint as "My own daughter Catherine." Matt was greatly taken by this I gathered that he would regard it as the greatest favour imaginable to be so addressed.

Mr O'Callaghan also stated that Matt once told him that it cost him more to give up tobacco than to give up drink. Asked by Mr O'Callaghan as to whether he ever had any remarkable spiritual experience Matt replied "only once." Questioned further he said that he was called out of his sleep and a voice told him to pray for a fellow-workman whom he had for a long time been trying to convert. The man died unexpectedly that night.

The following, in Mr Raphael O'Callaghan's handwriting, is a document he handed in to the 1931 Tribunal:

> There was nothing striking or impressive in Matt Talbot's appearance. To meet him on his daily rounds he was a very commonplace type of working-man, poorly clad, but clean. He was somewhat below middle height, of slight and wiry build, he walked rapidly, with long strides and loose, swinging gait. His bearing indicated recollection rather than preoccupation.
>
> Meeting him at close quarters, one was at once struck by the high forehead and rounded temples. His eyes were large, with drooping lids which gave his face a serious, thoughtful expression ... His topics of conversation were nearly always of a religious nature, and on the rare occasions when he referred to social or political questions, he simply stated the views of others as he had heard them at his daily work ... He had a retentive memory and could quote appropriate passages and incidents bearing on matters discussed. His strong points seemed to be a certain native wit which enabled him to get hold of his subject with a personal grip which made him sure of his ground.*

---

*Mr O'Callaghan was Matt's "great personal friend" mentioned by Sir Joseph Glynn in The Life of Matt Talbot (pp. 77-78). Mr O'Callaghan explained Matt's ability to read and understand books beyond the grasp of an uneducated man: "The explanation seemed to me to lie in his clear, logical mind. He was convinced that if the truths of Revelation, as regards the Incarnation and Redemption were accepted as true, there should be no limit to our service save the impossible. This view urged him on to his life of extreme penance and enabled him to persevere to the end."

Mr O'Callaghan also supplied a list of the books he lent to Matt Talbot between 1912 and 1925: Butler's *Lives of Saints*, 12 Vols; *Growth in Holiness* (Faber); *Watches of the Passion* (Fr Galwey, S.J.); *The Catholic Doctrine of Grace* (Joyce); *Doctrine of the Incarnation* (St Thomas Aquinas); *Holy Communion* (Dalgairns); *Temporal Mission of the Holy Ghost* (Manning); *England and the Sacred Heart* (Price); *Ortus. Christi* (Mother St Paul); *Meditations on the Mysteries of the Holy Rosary* (Père Monsabre, O.P.); *Catholic Mysticism* (Algar Thorold); *Catechism, Doctrinal, Moral, etc.* (Power); *Christian Inheritance* (Dr Hedley) *Catechism of the Council of Trent; Modern Infidelity Exposed* (Robertson); *Miniature Lives of the Saints*, 2 Vols (Bowden); *Anima Devota* (Fr Pagnini); *History of the Bible* (Reeves); *Large Life of St Vincent de Paul* (Bougard); *Study of Lost and Saved* (Fr Walsh, S.J.); *Present Position of Catholics* (Newman); *Ancient Irish Church* (Fr Gaffney, O.P.); *Maria Corona* (Canon Sheehan); *The Creator and the Creature* (Faber); *The Blessed Sacrament* (Faber).

Besides the *Life of St Catherine of Siena* (2 vols) by Drane, already mentioned, Mr O'Callaghan also lent Matt Talbot *Lives of St Patrick, St Elizabeth of Hungary; St Laurence O'Toole; St Magdalen de Pazzi; Thomas à Kempis; Pius IX; Mother Marie of Jesus; Cardinal Manning; Cardinal Franzelin; Father Faber* and others.

Mr Paddy Laird, an employee of T. & C. Martin's, in an interview, recalled the days when he and his father often walked home with Matt from work in the evenings. Mr Laird confesses that he himself did not always relish the prospect, "for, the very evening you'd be in a hurry going somewhere, Matt would say 'We'll make a visit,' or maybe he wouldn't say anything at all, just go in to St Laurence O'Toole's, or Portland Row, and my father would go with him and I'd go, too. He would walk along home with us then. Some people have the idea that Matt would not chat, that he always went around in silence. That was not so; he was always very pleasant company—and enjoyed a laugh. He was a lot fonder of his sister Mary (Mrs Andrews) than of Susan (Mrs Fylan)." Paddy continued—

"He took an interest in whatever we'd be talking about coming up from work. In those days it was either politics, or the strikes, but sometimes the talk would be about football matches. Matt never went to matches, but he'd listen when you were describing the play, and he'd remember the names of the players and their teams and whenever the next game came in which those players figured he'd ask how they had played. Not, I believe now, that he had any interest himself in sport, but just to be affable and good company. And, though he would never allow bad language to go unchecked, he used plenty of harmless slang. I don't remember well now what exactly were the slang expressions used then, but I do remember Matt having picked up one of them and he used it long after it had gone out of date. It was—'Ah, go and get your hair cut'—when anyone was trying to rush him at the loading or unloading of the timber he'd say that—in a jolly sort of way. If you asked him to buy a ticket for anything, he always would, but he'd ask a day's grace to bring the money, because he never carried money. He told my father (the late Mr Bob Laird) the reason for this.

Shortly after his conversion, he said, he was passing a public house—Mr Bushe's, I think—at the top of Gardiner Street, and he was terribly tempted to break his pledge. He went up and down past the public-house two or three times, feeling the money in his pocket, and getting more and more anxious for the drink. Finally, he couldn't bear it any longer and went in; there wasn't anyone there who knew him and he was not known to the men serving behind the bar. For some reason, though he waited a long time, no one came to him to ask his order and, suddenly, he turned on his heel and went out and on to Gardiner Street Church, a minute's walk away. He remained there praying until it closed and he told my father that he made a resolution never again to carry money with him, in case the same temptation seized him.

That Matt never carried money is a fact; if approached by some of his fellow-workers who were selling tickets for charity, or making a collection for someone who was ill, Matt would agree to subscribe but would ask them to wait till the following day as he had no money on him; he never failed to remember the subscription. Mr McGuirk and Mr Fuller said that he always subscribed to the various workers' funds but always asked a day's grace before bringing the money required. Later he left a sum of money in charge of the office at the timber yard and, when he was requested to give something to any fund or charity, drew money from the amount set aside for this purpose.

Those who knew him calculated that ten shillings a week was the sum total expended by Matt Talbot on rent and the necessities of life. Anything he had over he gave to charity. During his mother's lifetime, that is, up to 1915, he gave her £1 a week, almost all his wages up to the 1913 strike period. For the rest of his life, though his wages rose to £3 1s. 6d. weekly, he managed to live on about 10s.; an increase in wages simply meant, for him, something extra to give in charity.

Mr O'Connor, of Martin's, told that Matt Talbot made a practice of attending every charity sermon preached in the city and suburbs and that he never went to those services with less than a pound-note. On one Sunday there was a sermon being preached in a church in a rather select locality where a very popular preacher had been asked to make the appeal. When Matt arrived the church was packed to the doors, though it was before the hour for the 12 o'clock Mass, at which the sermon was to be given. After trying to gain admittance, Matt, his pound-note in his hand, saw some people still getting in by one entrance, where a collector was making a sixpenny admission charge. Matt went round there. The collector said, "Sixpence, this door." Matt, not wishing to "break" the donation he had for the collection, explained that he had brought no change. The collector—who, perhaps, had seen the pound-note and concluded that the man seeking admission was just trying to get in without paying—said, "Well, you can't get in here." Remarking quietly, "It's the house of God," Matt turned aside, remaining in the porch for Mass and listening carefully to the sermon. One wonders if the collector on the door saw the other collection taken up, and noted the contribution given by the man to whom he had refused admission.

Mr Edward Fuller relates that several times Matt gave men in Martin's "the price of a pair of boots." Mr Michael McGuirk remembers that once Matt gave his (Mr McGuirk's) brother the price of a drink, remarking that "a pint of porter never did anyone any harm." He did not, however, give money for drink to men whom he knew to be in the habit of taking too much. A Mrs Leavy, who lived in Rutland Street, in the period between 1912 and Matt's death, relates that her husband, Patrick Leavy, was going to get work in the Isle of Man in 1914, having been unemployed since the time of the Big Strike. The Leavy family were very badly off, and Mrs Leavy asked Matt could he help them. He lent them £3; after a long time Mrs Leavy found herself able to start making repayments, but Matt would not take the money. Mr Francis Donnellan, who lived in the same house as Matt Talbot from 1909 to 1925, testified:

> Sometime after World War I, about 1919 or 1920, while I was on strike, he came to see me; we had some conversation about religion and he asked me if I ever read religious books ... He added, "You have a young family here, and you must be hard pressed—if you want a few pounds I'll give them to you." I did not accept the money then as I thought that the strike would not last long; he told me to apply to him later if I found I needed it.

Another witness, Mr Carew, a foreman in T. & C. Martin's, related that a priest (from Monaghan, Mr Fuller said) came to the yard and asked permission to make a collection from the men. Mr Carew told him to put up a notice saying that he would call on pay-day and would take donations from those who wished to help the charity for which he was collecting. On the Friday, when the men were paid, the priest returned and made his collection; when he was leaving, Mr Carew asked him if he had been up with Matt Talbot—indicating where Matt was and knowing that Matt would be a certain subscriber. The priest went back to Matt and then came to Mr Carew, saying that he scrupled taking what the last man had given. Mr Carew asked, "How much did he give?" and the priest replied, "All he had about him." As Matt had just received his pay-packet containing £3 1s. 6d., Mr Carew thought that he handed over the whole amount.

On one occasion he gave a sum of £5 to Father T. Murphy, S.J., in Gardiner Street. Brother Furlong, S.J., told that Matt sometimes gave him offerings of four or five shillings to buy flowers for Our Blessed Lady's altar; after some time he ceased giving this money, remarking, "I will give it to the missions." Collectors for various religious houses, for shrines in city churches, for the Society of St Vincent de Paul, and other charities, all knew Matt Talbot, if not by name at least by sight, and he gave them regular and generous subscriptions. Towards his last years he seemed to concentrate all his charity on the Missions—on one Foreign Mission Society in particular. He also seems to have been sending, over very many years, subscriptions to the Poor Clares of Keady. Leaflets sent him in acknowledgement by the nuns appear in his books from the early 1900s. A search in the Convent records did not show the name Matt Talbot, but donations sent by "a friend" in Dublin came up again and again. Matt must have sent this money through someone else, as he not infrequently did in the case of other charities: he was not, it will be remembered, much of a letter writer.

CHAPTER X

THE YEAR 1913 SAW THE NOT UNEXPECTED clash between Capital and Labour in Dublin. Matt Talbot, being one of the workers to come out when called upon during the "Great Strike," a brief survey of the conditions and events that led to the strike is essential for the understanding of the lives of the men among whom Matt worked daiiy. An inquiry published by the British Board of Trade in 1912, shows that food prices rose by 14% between 1905 and 1912. But the wages did not rise to meet the increase in the cost of living. The late Seumas O'Farrell, writing on this period in an article in *Studies,* gave the anwer to the obvious question: What did the workers do?

> They ate less and they repatched their garments. There was nothing else they could do. State assistance, reluctantly given and after imposing degrading conditions, consisted of admission to the Poor House or relief in kind.

> "Relief in kind," or, as it was all too familiarly known, Outdoor Relief, consisted of a few loaves of bread, a pinch of tea, a small dole of sugar, a few ounces of margarine. To get it, the recipient had to go personally to the Poor House and present a ticket issued by the Relieving Officer. On it a widow and her children had to exist or die. Rent was met by a charitable organisation, the Poor House being the only shelter the State was willing to provide. The pennies of neighbours buried the dead. They suffered, God knows, and suffered in silence. The law-givers were far away in Westminster, concerned with the demand for Home Rule. The slum owners were represented in the Dublin

Corporation. To whom could they appeal? To Caesar against Caesar?

The poor helped the poor when no other help was available. They gave the bread out of their own hungry mouths to those whose need was greater . . .75% of the working-class expenditure on food went to purchase essentials. Luxuries consisted, for those who bought them, of porter at two-pence a pint and cigarettes at five for a penny . . .How they lived was nobody's concern but their own. Where they lived was decided for them by the rent of a tenement room. Out of 16s. little remained to pay for shelter when a family had been even half-fed.

Dublin, as a manufacturing centre, lacked the advantages which the proximity of coal mines, iron deposits, great forests, and other raw materials afforded many big cities in the industrial world. On the other hand, the Irish capital had in the river which cut the city in two, an indubitable, if not fully utilised, asset. Dublin had also a plentiful supply of labour, too much, indeed, for the needs of its industries during the latter half of the 19th century and the early decades of the 20th. It was this disproportion of supply and demand in the labour market that constituted the city's gravest economic problem in the decades preceding the strike. Seumas O'Farrell has cited the wonderful fraternal charity of the Dublin poor during those years. An English journalist, Arnold Wright, gave the following summing-up of the Dublin working population in his book, *Disturbed Dublin,* written after a visit paid to the city to report on the strike.*

---

*Apropos of Arnold Wright, in the selection of James Connolly's writings edited by D. Ryan, a footnote to Connolly's essay on Mr. Wright's books states that the author was paid £500 by the Federated Employers of Dublin for writing *Disturbed Dublin.*

They (the Dublin workers) are strongly emotional and highly responsive to outside influences, they are easily caught up by any movement which appeals either to their pocket, their religious susceptibilities, or their sense of patriotism. Nowhere, perhaps, in the wide world is there more plastic material for moulding by the hands of the man who has a mission, or thinks he has, to reform humanity.

When the Sidney Webbs, G. B. Shaw's friends, came to visit Ireland, they stayed with Horace Plunkett at The Barn, his bungalow at Kilteragh, Foxrock. The Countess of Fingall (related by marriage to Horace Plunkett) was visiting Kilteragh at the same time. She recalled the occasion in her memoirs:

> The Sidney Webbs came and, true to their Socialism, would not change for dinner. They did a tour of Ireland, and Mrs. Webb came back to Kilteragh and reported: "They do not know the beginning of Socialism in this country. Every one of them is an individualist to his or her backbone."

> It was quite true. There is no natural Communism in the Irish character. Naturally secretive, the people will hide even their pigs and hens from each other.

As there were far more workers in the city than industry could absorb, wages for the workers classed as "unskilled" were low. A Government inquiry was held into Dublin Housing conditions in 1913, when the following figures were given in the report of the Committee: Of heads of families occupying tenement houses, 5,604 earned no more than 15s. a week; 9,000 earned from 15s. to £1; 2,585 earned £1 to 25s.; 1,627 earned 25s. to 30s.; and 2,384 over 30s. These men were all casual workers, working whenever they were taken on, at a busy time in the building industry, or at the docks; some were street traders, some held horses or did other catchpenny jobs. The general conclusion of the Committee was "that a large number of the labouring classes, van drivers, carters, messengers and such like, earn wages not in excess of 18s. a week."

The wretched accommodation and food within the purchasing power of this depressed group did not increase their value in the labour market. Indeed, it was a source of constant wonder to visitors, that in such an environment and under the constant pressure of want and misery, the poor of Dublin lived up to their religion with a devotion and a certain, almost fierce, tenacity found in few cities undergoing similar economic and industrial depression. These visitors did not know that the 1913 generation of Dublin workers were the children of a generation who had come unscathed through the campaign against the faith inaugurated in the 'fifties and carried on with unabating vigour right through the ensuing decades. Nor did they know that the Dublin poor of 1913 were the grandchildren and great-grandchildren of the Dubliners of the period following on Catholic Emancipation in 1829—the generation that during the hungry 'forties had built houses for God before they sought better shelter for themselves; to the poor Catholics of the latter decades of the century it was more important to hand on the faith than to hand on improved conditions of living. That could wait. But it could not wait forever.

The slums of Dublin, in 1913 and for long before, were—to quote Mr Wright again—"something apart in the inferno of social degradation."

Nowhere (he continues) can there be found concentrated so many of the evils which are associated with the underworld of our modern civilisation. To say that men and women live like the beasts of the field is the merest truth. In buildings—old, rotten and permeated with physical and moral corruption—they crowd in incredible numbers . . . .A fourteenth of the entire inhabitants of Dublin are living in dwellings admittedly unfit for human habitation, while about another eighth are housed in circumstances almost equally wretched . . . Nearly a third of the population live under conditions which are injurious to physique and morality.

Father Peter Monaghan, a curate in St Nicholas of Myra's, Francis Street, who gave evidence to this Housing Committee of 1913, mentioned one tenement known to him in which 107 people lived and in which there were only two water-closets for the entire building, and for both sexes. Corporation officials challenged Father Monahan's figures, stating that only 95 lived in that particular tenement and that there were three, not two w.c.'s!

Another witness at this Commission was the Treasurer of the N.S.P.C.C., who spoke of the children of the slum areas "thronging the thoroughfares, under no control, running moral and physical risks." This man, in all his experience, "never once saw a woman in the tenements sewing or knitting," though there were rents and tatters in plenty.

Overcrowding and unemployment was in Dublin a vicious circle. In 1911, as many as 169,736 persons were listed as "the indefinite and non-productive class"; and 45,169 were classed as "unskilled labour"—about one-seventh of the city's population. It was this forty-five thousand and their families—a third of Dublin's population—who lived in and paid for the rooms unfit for human habitation. They were the people doomed for life to the shifting sands of insecurity, the people with no hope of ever rising out of the degradation of their surroundings. Courage did not come to them until Conolly came; they did not rouse themselves until they heard Jim Larkin.

Unrest was in the air. There were strikes in other countries. English and Scottish industrial centres experienced work stoppages. The movement to which Arthur Griffith and his friends were pledged was being spoken of—but quietly, because of the enemy within the gates. It was a long cry since '98 and Lord Edward and Emmet, since '48 and the Young Irelanders, since '67 and the Fenians. No leader came after Parnell.

Despite his miserable surroundings, the Dublin slum-dweller impressed Arnold Wright:

> He is certainly not vicious with the viciousness of the low Londoner. There is no Dublin equivalent of the Paris Apache; it is doubtful whether there are many genuine hooligans. People in the Dublin slums do not stare and gibe at the well-dressed stranger as they would in the low parts of the East End of London. There was never a case of death from starvation in the Irish capital . . . it is undeniable that there is an immense amount of kindly feeling for the misfortunes of others in those drab, dreary streets. How good the poor are to each other was testified to by nearly all the expert witnesses at a recent inquiry. Indeed, it is the slum-dwellers' abiding sense of the virtues of charity which leads to the worst over-crowding in the tenement houses, for a family occupying a room never seems so large that it cannot take another which has been evicted for non-payment of rent or some other cause.

163

In a paper dealing with the housing and living conditions of "unskilled labour" in Dublin, which he read before the Statistical and Social Enquiry Society of Ireland, in 1914, Mr G. Chart, M.A., stated:

The Dublin labouring class is deeply religious, as is shown by many indications. It lives, as a rule, a much more moral and respectable life than could be expected considering its surroundings. It exhibits, in a marked degree, the social virtues of kindness, cheerfulness and courtesy. The inquirers of the Housing and Town Planning Association, though they went into hundreds of dwellings during a great strike, and asked numbers of very pointed and delicate questions, rarely encountered suspicion or incivility. Mentally and morally, this class is probably on a higher level than the labouring classes of most cities.

The basic problem was that there was not sufficient employment for these 45,000 "unskilled" workers, on whom at least 100,000 depended for their daily bread. As "unskilled labour" was a drug on the market, it sold cheaply. And, this state of affairs having become chronic a third of the city's population lived in perpetual insecurity. For them the passing weeks were a see-saw on which they either sunk to utter destitution where the very needs of life were lacking, or rose to a meagre subsistence on the inadequate pay brought home by the wage-earner—if he *did* bring it home. One in every three of Dublin's 350,000 citizens belonged to this depressed—and often exploited—class.

As has been seen, efforts were being made to organise the unskilled and casual labourers of the city. In 1908 a number of Labour men in Dublin attempted to form a Union of Irish workers, but the attempt failed. Mr Jim Larkin broke with the Liverpool Union, of which he was Irish representative, and joined the Dublin and Cork workers, who were planning an Irish Union that would be independent of Labour organisations across the Channel. This was the beginning of the Irish Transport and General Workers' Union; to balance its numerical and financial weakness, it had Larkin for General Secretary.

From 1909 onwards the I.T.G.W.U. was engaged in a series of strikes and lock-outs; its funds were inadequate for the financing of these disputes, so it had to turn for help to the old Dublin Trades Council—the skilled workers' Union—and to raise funds by means of collections, lectures, raffles and dances. In 1910 James Connolly returned to Ireland from the United States and became Secretary for the Belfast branch of the I.T.G.W.U., and organiser of the Union for Ulster. But for the next few years relations between Connolly and Larkin were not of the best.

In a letter to William O'Brien, dated May 24th, 1911, Connolly wrote:

> Do not pay any attention to what Larkin says ... the man is utterly unreliable and dangerous because unreliable.

In a letter to Mr O'Brien, dated September 13th, 1912, Connolly again referred to Larkin:

> He does not seem to want a democratic Labour movement; he seems to want a Larkinite movement only .
> . .He must rule, or will not work, and in the present stage of the Labour movement he has us at his mercy. And he knows it, and is using his power unscrupulously, I regret to say . . . I am sick of all this playing to one man, but am prepared to advise it for the sake of the movement.

And in a letter dated July 29th, 1913:

> ....I don't think I can stand Larkin as a boss much longer. He is simply unbearable. He is forever snarling at me .... (Follows a list of grievances which Connolly said he suffered at the hands of Larkin.) .... I would formerly have trusted to his generosity in financial matters, now I would not trust him at all. He thinks he can use Socialists as he pleases, and then when his end is served, throw them out ... He will never get me to bow to him.

The Lenten Lectures in Gardiner Street in 1910 reflected the problems that beset Dubliners at that time; Father Robert Kane, S.J., gave six lectures on *Socialism;* his lectures were soon afterwards produced as a pamphlet. James Connolly, in an essay, *Labour, Nationality and Religion,* discussed these lectures, condemning them as an attack on Socialism. As a great many of the men in T. & C. Martin's Timber Yards were living in the Gardiner Street area, it is reasonable to assume that the lectures—and Connolly's criticism of them—came in for much discussion.

At least one man in Martin's bought Father Kane's pamphlets and studied them; having studied them he bought and studied others—all dealing with the questions that so closely concerned the Catholic workers of the time. The man, Matt Talbot, had a number of books and pamphlets which he was reading when Connolly and Larkin were levering the great body of ill-paid, unskilled labour into a position where they would be better placed to work themselves free of the morass of misery wherein they were stuck. When unfamiliar names like Marx and Engels were being quoted by workers who knew little of either one or the other, one Dublin workman was making himself—and perhaps others—acquainted with the teaching of the Church on such questions as Capital, Labour, a Just Wage, Strikes and similar questions that affected underpaid casual workers—questions that were for workers the burning topics of the time.

Among those booklets were: *An Examination of Socialism* (Belloc) 1909; *The Church and Socialism* (Belloc) 1909; *Francisco Ferrer and the Spanish Anarchists; A Catholic Social Catechism.*

Larger books being read by Matt in 1912 and 1913 included *The Social Value of the Gospel* (Leon Garriguet); this book cost him 10s. and he had marked it at a section dealing with Communism in the Early Church. *The Catholic Social Year Book for 1913* was another purchase; he had marked that at Catholic Social Action in South America; Pope Leo XIII's letter on *The Condition of the Working Classes*; another Catholic Social Catechism, published in 1913, in which the following portions were marked: The Patient; The Sickness; The Cause of the Malady; Unlicensed Practitioners; Famous Doctor's Remedy; Applying the Remedy.

Father Lambert McKenna, S.J., had a series of pamphlets published about this time; of these Matt bought three: *The Church and Working Men; The Church and the Working Guild; The Church and the Trade Unions.*

To suggest, as has been done, that Matt Talbot took no interest in his fellow-workers' struggle for justice, is absurd. Apart from his reading at this critical time, there is the evidence of his comrades in T. & C. Martin's. Before giving this evidence, the history of the Big Strike of 1913 must be recapitualated.

Mention has been made of the series of strikes that took

167

place in the capital from the beginning of the century; these strikes increased in number in the years subsequent to 1908, when the I.T.G.W.U. was formed; from this time, too, the sympathetic strike gained popularity, and labour stoppages were frequent. Jim Larkin was writing fiery articles in the *Irish Worker* in which the Scabs, the Capitalists, the Dublin Metropolitan Police (this "savage breed of Cossacks") were accused, abused and disparaged, week in, week out. In 1911 Larkin tried to close the gaps between the classes of workers; in particular he took up the cause of the dockers; a series of stoppages of work took place and finally the employers in their turn formed the Dublin Employers Federation—immediately dubbed by Larkin the "Employers' Secret Society."

The Viceroy, the Earl of Aberdeen, called a meeting, inviting Jim Larkin and another I.T.G.W.U. representative to a conference with two of the Employers' Union members in the Castle. A temporary truce resulted, but a few weeks afterwards a dispute broke out between the Union and the timber merchants; on this occasion the railwaymen were called out, when they refused to handle timber consignments. The strike lasted for some weeks in the early autumn of 1911, but petered out when the Amalgamated Society of Railway servants decided that they were fighting a losing battle and that to pay out more strike money from already depleted funds was to ruin their Society. The following year saw further disputes—all involving large bodies of workers—when Jacob's Biscuit Factory, various Shipping Companies, and firms engaged in engineering and building were held up some by one, some by several strikes. Thus things continued until the Horse Show Week of 1913—a series of skirmishes, major and minor, all leading up to the battle-royal.

Mr Murphy, Chairman of the Tramway Company, owner of Independent Newspapers, with business interests in West Africa and various British cities, decided that his transport company would, for the future, employ no I.T.G.W.U. member. Other employers followed this lead and there were lock-outs in several concerns all over the city, the numbers of those thus thrown out of employment soon reaching the 30,000 mark. The Press, with the exception of the I.T.G.W.U. organ, the *Irish Worker,* was antagonistic to the men on strike; at mass meetings in Sackville—now O'Connell—Street, there were clashes between the strikers and the police. The latter had their own old scores to settle with the Union men; they were still smarting from the castigating they had received in the *Irish Worker,* when not only had they been collectively stigmatized as "skulking bullies," "gigantic columns of ignorance," and worse, but had been attacked individually, names and numbers of certain over-officious policemen being given in Larkin's paper, with particulars of alleged offences, proving the anti-worker animus of these constables.

The worst encounter between the strikers and the police took place on August 30th, continuing into the 31st, when the constabulary, some drunk, some out-of-hand, and all seemingly under a misapprehension as to the functions of a police force, attacked a block of tenements in Corporation Street and Foley Street, batoning strikers and non-strikers alike, beating up women and children, and wrecking the humble homes and the poor belongings of the unfortunate people living in that area. Beresford Place and Ringsend saw further baton-charges and riots; Redmond's Hill was the scene of a hand-to-hand battle between the crowds and the police on August 31st, resulting in over a hundred casualties.

The funeral of a young man who died as a result of the O'Connell Street incident—coming as it did on the heels of a disaster in Church Street, when two tenements collapsed killing seven persons and seriously injuring many others—brought the city to the verge of a workers' revolution. Some firms closed down; others threatened to do so; the Port of Dublin was in danger of being closed. Hurriedly, the Lord Mayor, Mr Lorcan Sherlock, tried to arrange a conference of both parties to the dispute, but the Employers' Union simply dug in their heels and refused to employ any I.T.G.W.U. member; they also drafted an Agreement Form for workers, one clause of which asked that the latter agree to handle and deliver all goods from any source whatever. As this was a direct onslaught on the Union "sympathetic strike" tactics, several firms whose men were not already on strike, now found themselves involved. One of these firms was Martin's, where the men refused to sign the agreement; among those who came out on strike at T. & C. Martin's was Matt Talbot.

It has been stated more than once, and publicly, that Matt Talbot was a strike-breaker who took no interest in his fellow-workers' struggle for better conditions. This is not true. Apart from the evidence of men who worked with him and others who met him during the strike, documents still preserved by his Union utterly disprove this allegation. Matt joined the Builders-Labourers' Branch, the No. 1 Branch of the I.T. & G.W.U. on 22 September 1911 and was a fully paid-up member when the 1913 strike began. He paid the strike levy. He did not carry a picket but neither did he pass one; men in his age-bracket, those nearing sixty, were not asked to picket. If he had 'scabbed' during the strike would not his Union have expelled him? Yet, his name remained on the books and his Branch paid him National Health Insurance benefit during his illness of 1923-24. At a meeting held a few years after the big strike workers shouted down a speaker who called Matt a strike-breaker.

A lot has been made of his non-attendance at Union meetings, especially during the strike; but he never read newspapers, never raised his eyes walking along a street to notice hoardings or posters and he spent his entire day in the church; it is possible that he did not know of the meetings. Even today, when the labour movement is highly organised, well educated and articulate members often fail to show up at ordinary and special meetings of their Branch. Not everyone is meeting-minded.*

At the Enquiries the following evidence was given concerning Matt Talbot during the 1913 strike period:

Mr John Robbins:

>He was a conscientious workman and even anxious for work if it were not his duty. I never heard him speak against his employers, but he knew quite well that the men were not always sufficiently paid. He once said that Mr X. (a foreman) was "an employers' man," i.e., leaning more towards the employers than to us men. Matt did not picket

---

*In 1960 a Yugo-Slav Jesuit was arrested and charged with "subversive activities". He was accused of having preached on Matt Talbot and of telling the congregation that Matt went on strike in 1913. As in other Communist countries, strikes are banned in Yugo-Slavia and constitute a "crime against the State". At the priest's trial the Public Prosecutor declared that "the life-story of the Irish worker, Matt Talbot, who regarded the Church as favourable to strikes, was bound to undermine the Yugo-Slav social and political system". Our Eastern Comrades do not regard Matt as a "scab".

when the Big Strike was on. He did not speak much of the workers' troubles but he was in favour of the claim for fair pay for a fair day's work.

Mr Raphael O'Callaghan:

Matt Talbot talked very freely with me about the labour situation and the strike. The subject was a delicate one inasmuch as he was a striker while I was an employer of labour and a member of the Employer' Federation with which the strike leaders were at war. I especially admired his tact in these conversations; the bitterness of the controversies of that time was entirely absent from what he said and he tried not to hurt my feelings, but he held his own opinion and could do so well. He was pleased that the men, who had undeniably been underpaid, got increased wages, yet he kept himself detached from the high feeling prevalent in the city and was not caught up in the general excitement. He certainly did not allow it to interfere with his spiritual life and Matt Talbot's joy in his increased wages was because he was able to contribute more to charities, especially the foreign missions. I heard that he had hot words with a Miss ——— about the strike; he had some Larkinite literature. He did not picket, nor did he go for any strike pay. The men themselves brought it to him. Before the strike his wages were fifteen shillings a week; it was on this account that my aunt asked me to give him some clothes.

Rev. Brother Furlong, S.J., also mentioned Matt's disagreement with the formidable Miss ———:

Miss ——— had always been a bit antagonistic to Matt. She remarked to me during the strike that she did not wonder that Matt Talbot was on the side of the strikers; she said: "He is a Socialist and has a Socialist Catechism in his pocket."

Very Rev. Fr J. J. Canon Flood, the late P.P. of Holy Name Parish, Beechwood Avenue, gave evidence:

I did not know Matt Talbot personally but I was Curate in St Laurence O'Toole's Church from 1908 to 1924 and I distinctly remember a strange figure of a man who always seemed to be in a hurry; he wore a workman's clothes and was spare and ascetic-looking and seemed insufficiently fed. He ran rather than walked. I did not then know him as Matt Talbot but have since identified him. He came into the church every evening and remained about fifteen minutes and he also came in the mornings arriving about the middle of Mass . . .Since Matt's death I have only heard one person who spoke against him and that was an extremist agitator. At a meeting he referred to Matt as a "strike breaker"; the audience, composed of men of rather extreme views, protested and compelled the speaker to withdraw his remarks.

Mr James Tallon, a tailor, stated:

The big strike of 1913 troubled me. I asked Matt what were the rights of it. He said that it had troubled him also and that he spoke to a priest in Gardiner Street who gave him a book to read. On the third or fourth page he read that no one had the right to starve the poor into submission; he told me that that was enough for him and settled his conscience.

Mr Frank Larkin spoke of Matt's regard for Jim Larkin:

Matt had a great regard for Larkin and for anyone who strove for the good of others; he felt that Larkin had been let down by the men afterwards and spoke of the ingratitude shown by the workers towards their leader.

Mr John Gunning testified as follows;

During the 1913 strike Matt did not take strike pay unless it was brought to him. As I was in good employment then—I was a silver polisher in Messrs West's—I pressed him to take a loan from me. After considerable pressing he took sums in all amounting to about £4 or £5. When the strike was over he repaid me at the rate of 5s. a week.

An old lady, Mrs Halbert, giving evidence at the first Tribunal, said that she knew Matt Talbot for about twenty-five years prior to his death in 1925. She used to attend the earliest Masses in St Francis Xavier's Church and when she arrived at the church before the hour when the doors were opened, she always found Matt Talbot there, "kneeling on the steps in hail, rain, snow or mud," saying his prayers while he waited. Mrs Halbert also stated:

> I used to have arguments with Matt Talbot about strikes, to which I was altogether opposed. On the occasion of the big strike he thought the men had a real grievance and he was altogether in their favour.

A Mrs Booker stated:

> The only time I saw Matt very annoyed was once when a woman insisted on speaking to Brother Furlong in the Jesuit Church. He (Matt) said to me, "The idea of delaying that man who has so much to do!" The woman overheard him and said, "And the idea of that old Larkinite—meaning Matt—speaking like that about me!"

Mr M. J. Dillon, a foreman in Martin's, made the following statement:

> Matt had a peculiar faculty of taking things quietly and yet of never being behind-hand or late with his work. You could not hustle him. He was respectful to his employers but did not hesitate to state his rights directly but respectfully. When the big strike was on Matt's attitude was that he himself was not badly treated but that his fellow-workers were badly paid. His sense of justice took in both employers and employed . . . One day at work, while there was a spell between lorries being loaded, he retired as usual to pray. When loading commenced again the gang had to go on without Matt as he did not turn up. He came along after a few minutes and I rebuked him,

saying that he should not waste his employers' time to say his prayers. He seemed very upset, apologised to me and said he had not heard the lorry returning and that it would not happen again. He kept his promise. When the men received a special allowance for unloading a ship, Matt would not claim his. As it was part of my duty to pay this money and it upset my accounts when one man failed to claim I spoke to him about it. He said "'Tis true we have to work a little harder, but then I have many a slack moment in the yard between loadings—I do not think I am entitled to this money." As he failed to come to me for it after that I used to keep it and when I met him would give him whatever had accumulated. He agreed to take it then, but said "I will give it to a charity."

His objection to taking the extra pay was because the other workers who got smaller weekly wages than he did and who had harder work to do only got the same bonus as himself when a ship was unloaded.

Mr Gethin, a commercial clerk in Martin's, gave further information regarding this "bonus" which Matt refused:

This money was not given for overtime but as a bonus to the men when a ship had to be cleared to catch the tide. If it caught the tide the men got a bonus of 2s. each. if it did not they only got their ordinary day's pay. They would have to work very hard to enable the ship to be unloaded in time to catch the tide.

Matt got on well with his employers but he could not be obsequious to any man; he showed proper respect but he was independent-minded and spoke out straight. When I was stocktaking Matt would have to remain on at the works on a Saturday. When finished I would say, "Well, that's the end, Matt," and he would reply "There's an end to everything except the one thing." Sometimes he used ask me if I thought I would live forever. There was not much *bonhomie* about Matt, but he was not uncheerful.

He was too unworldly to make the sort of jolly companion I used to prefer. He spoke to me of some of his pious practices but warned me to keep them secret; he wanted to make me a "saint" too, but I'm afraid he has not succeeded. The men held him in the highest regard and when he was in failing health they made up a collection for him and took it to him.

Mr Michael McGuirk said in evidence:

Matt did not have much to say about strikes. In the case of the 1913 strike, he was prepared to go with the majority of the men. Matt used to pay his strike money, but he never took an active part in pickets or strike meetings. He never discussed the questions of wages or the workers' rights with me.

All the men had a very good opinion of him . . . I believe they would have asked him for advice on occasion. I know he was never asked to picket like others and I know that he was on the side of the working man. He could occasionally get "worked up" in arguing about certain matters, but if he ever went away "heated" after an argument, he would return again either to apologise or to talk about something else . . . The men regarded him highly. They might have a joke about him, as they passed him at work—he was a good workman—but they respected him. I never heard of him having any rows either with his fellow-workmen or with his foreman. Matt was not a "boss's" man.

Mat was not asked to picket or to take part in any of the strike demonstrations, and the men did not even ask him to come for his strike pay—they brought it to him.*

Mr Edward (Ted) Fuller stated:

His fellow-workers in Martin's had a very high opinion of Matt; I never knew any of them to laugh or jibe at him. Matt told me, apropos of the rights of the working man,

---

*A shop steward, William McCarthy, of Buckingham Buildings, brought it to him.

that he admired any man who stood up for his rights. Regarding the 1913 strike, he told me that he was convinced that the men were deserving of higher wages than they were getting—he was in sympathy with them, but I never knew him to be at any strike meetings, nor did I hear that he was at such meetings: he did not picket with the other men, as he was not present at meetings when men were detailed to picket. He told me afterwards that during the strike he spent his time in the church saying his prayers and reading the Lives of the Saints. During the labour troubles he mentioned to me that the men were only looking for their rights. I cannot recall any instance where he himself stood up for his rights. Matt's sentiments were that the workers were entitled to higher wages. He always believed that a man should do a fair day's work for the wages he received. The men found it a pleasure to work with him; he was always so cheerful and agreeable.

Rev. Brother Furlong, S.J.:

The Servant of God was on the side of the workman, whom he wanted to see fairly treated. One morning I asked him if the strike (1913) had been settled yet. He said that it had not and added: "I hope they will get what they are looking for—a fair wage."

Miss ——— had a poor opinion of Matt Talbot.* She used to say that he was a Socialist and a Communist and had their Catechism in his pocket. I did not pay any attention to what she said as she was eccentric. She was the only person I ever heard saying a word against Matt or disagreeing with the general opinion that he was a very holy man . . . On the occasion of the appointment of the first Governor-General of the Irish Free State, I remember that, one morning Matt said to me: "Isn't it a terrible thing to have that man up there in the Park with £10,000 a year, and poor people starving?" I remarked: "Well, the

---

* Cf. page 174

poor we have always with us." Matt smiled at me and walked away.

Mr Francis Donnellan who lived in the same house as Matt Talbot for many years and whom Matt had helped during the strike, stated:

Very few people in our street knew Matt Talbot—he kept very much to himself. A Mr McKeag, a Protestant, who worked at Martin's, told me that when the men's language became very bad, Matt would take a large crucifix from his pocket, hold it up and say, "Look, boys, see who you are insulting." In time, Mr McKeag said, Matt acquired such an influence over his fellow-workers, that they never used bad language in his presence. He never discussed the strike or social questions with me. He used to say: "I do not know enough to judge—Jim Larkin knows best."

The late Mr William J. Larkin brother of Frank, said in evidence:

The conditions of the working men were very bad at the time of the 1913 strike. Matt was aware of this injustice. He came out on strike in 1913 with his fellow-workers, but did not take any active part in picketing. I knew him at the time and would say that he was in constant contact with his Trade Union during the strike. The other men did not blame him for not taking a more active part in the dispute—they respected him. There was no doubting his preparedness to act in accordance with the Church's teaching . . . He did not seem to be interested in temporal things . . . . A favourite phrase of his was: "It's all in God's hands." He co-operated with those who sought better conditions for the workers.

My opinion is that in matters arising at Trade Union Meetings, Matt would leave the decision to persons more competent than himself—he preferred too, to spend his time in prayer and meditation. In questions of justice arising at his place of employment, he would not hesitate to tell even his boss what he thought of him. He respected the authority of the Church, in spite of the fact that the atmosphere in Dublin then was not altogether favourable to the Church. He would come to the aid of a fellow-worker in need by giving money, the he himself had not much of this world's goods. A poor man since dead told me that Matt Talbot was an extraordinary man in his manner of helping others; he said that whenever "the little man (Matt) gave me anything, he would not wait for me to thank him, but ran away."

After Sodality Meetings in Gardiner Street Church, I got the impression that when Matt called some poor fellow aside and walked along the corridor (several of the church exits open on a long corridor running the length of the building) with him, it was either to give him some money or to convert him. I do not know whether he gave away all his wages, but I am certain that he helped the poor and many Catholic charities ... He had a winning way of leading others back to God. He hated pretence—he spoke with bluntness and frankness. He always gave everybody his due—I never knew him to do an injustice to anybody or to say an unkind word of another. He loved truth. He was not servile; but he served God.

Mrs Johnson, niece of Matt Talbot:

During the 1913 strike Matt took no part in picketing, as the men did not expect him to. Whenever I would try to introduce politics into the conversation he would say to me, raising his hand: "no politics—mind God, and no politics." Even though he took no active part in the strike, I always heard him say that the workmen had a right to a just wage. He never read a newspaper. He used to pray for people who were in trouble and he helped people in need of material assistance.

Mr Edward Carew, a foreman at Martin's:

I came to know Matt Talbot immediately after the 1913 strike. I heard that he was sympathetic with the men; he considered that they had a fair case. He did not picket with the other men, and, as far as I know, the others did not mind this—of course, he was getting on in years at the time. He got on well with his employers; he was respectful but not servile. He was prepared to fight his corner when justice was at stake. He was a good, religious, conscientious man who, in all these things, would have done what he thought was right. Mr Murphy, who was foreman in Martin's before my time, told me that Matt was offered another job in Martin's with higher pay; he refused the job. It is my impression that he refused the job because he did not like working with men who used bad language.

Although Mr Carew did not say so, his last sentence implies that the change of position would have meant that Matt would be among men addicted to using bad language. The witness also testified:

He used to lend money to men who needed help. I heard this from some of the men whom Matt helped. He never spoke about his good deeds. He was strict with himself, but quiet, kind and gentle with others. Everybody was fond of him; he had no enemies—all respected him. He never "played-up" to people, but spoke his mind frankly. He was not hot-headed, but solid and sensible; he was a diligent workman who did his work faithfully and did not waste his time. I never could find fault with his work and I never knew him to disobey an order. He did good turns for others whenever he could. I remember one instance in which I heard him saying to Mr Murphy, the former foreman, that he was sorry for some hot words they had. Mr Murphy said: "That's all right, Matty . . ." He had an extraordinary influence over and power of handling men who were inclined to be bullies—an influence such as I could never exercise myself.

I heard that he once refused to obey an order because it was against his conscience; he was prepared to lose his job sooner than do whatever it was he regarded as not right; he said "he had his soul's interests to consider first."

On one occasion a director of T. & C. Martin's asked Matt if he had seen another worker, who had come in late. Matt replied: "I wish you would not ask me these questions, you know I do not wish to answer them." When the director had passed on, Matt turned to the culprit, who had been hiding nearby, and remarked: "Do you hear that? Attend to it. I will not tell lies to save you." On another occasion, he spoke to a foreman with a certain freedom and maintained his own opinion: for this the foreman rebuked him. Next day Matt came back and apologised, saying that Our Lord had told him to do so.

In his evidence, Sir Joseph Glynn said that from interviews he had, soon after Matt's death with foremen and others at Martin's, he would say that Matt Talbot thought that the labourers of his time, particularly the married men, were underpaid; he used to speak with warmth on these matters. On one occasion when everyone in the yard except Matt and one other got a rise, Matt Talbot presented himself at the Managing Director's office and asked for an increase of wages, or an explanation of why he had received no increase when everyone else did. The manager said: "You don't call yourself a workman," and refused the increase. Matt left without comment.

Mr Fuller relates that once when a fellow-worker spoke to Matt about his master, meaning one of the Mr Martin's, Matt said: "He is not my master—he is only my boss; I have only one Master—in Heaven." He was always straightforward and courageous and often said: "I have only one Master, God Almighty."

Mr McGuirk told the Judges of how, on one occasion, Matt was in his usual secluded corner between stacks of timber, praying as was his custom between loading times. Mr Thomas Martin and a distinguished visitor came in and Mr Martin heard some movement among the timber, and called: "Come out, whoever is there, and don't be afraid." Matt walked out and said: "With all respects to you, sir, I never yet met a man that I was afraid of." Mr Martin said nothing, but walked away. Later he told Sir Joseph Glynn that Matt Talbot would always speak his mind when the occasion called for it—that his demeanour towards the firm's principals was always respectful but frank; "Matt would always tell you what he thought."

But, although Matt took no public and active part in the workers' struggle, one of his brothers did. When after the grim winter of 1913-1914, the English Unions refused to send further financial support to the Dublin strikers, and the latter, faced with no other alternative but starvation, had to return to work on the employers' terms, men who had take a prominent part in the struggle were, in many cases refused re-employment. One of Matt's brothers was among these—Mr Fuller thinks it was Joe, Charlie, the shoe-shiner having died in 1908, as is clear from the following entry in Matt's handwriting in one of his books:

Charles Talbot, who died 8th June, 1908. May the Lord have mercy on his soul.

The aftermath of mutual mistrust and antagonism between employers and employed continued for long after the strike. And Matt Talbot continued reading up the controversial questions raised by the dispute. Men in T. & C. Martin's told how, on one occasion, an argument arose at the men's dinner-hour about the Church's stand on some social question; someone suggested, "Ask Matt." Matt was accordingly fetched along and the question was put to him. He replied: "I don't know the correct answer to that; but I know where to find it; I heard of a book recently published where that is dealt with. But I"ll have to send to America for the book." He went away; those who had called for him were a bit disappointed; those who first raised the question, a little jubilant. If Matt had not the Church's answer, who had?

A couple of months afterwards, when all concerned had forgotten the incident, Matt joined the group of men at their dinner-hour, rather to their surprise, for it was an accepted fact that Matt should spend the time praying in between the timber-stacks. He had a new, well-bound book in his hands; *Democratic Industry*, by Dr Joseph Husslein, S.J. The publishers were P. J. Kennedy and Sons, New York. This purchase cost Matt about 12s. 6d. He had marked the following sections: The Origin of the Medieval Guilds; A Scotch Merchant Guild; The First Modern Labour Class; Woman and Child Labour; Social Insurance.

Other items acquired by Matt at this period included a pamphlet of Dr Coffey's, *Between Capitalism and Socialism;* and another by his friend, Dr Keane, O.P., *A Living Wage and a Family Wage.*

Matt Talbot said he did not understand the problems raised by the strike; though he gave time and study to the questions affecting the workers, he did not think himself qualified to give an opinion; he left decisions to others; he abided by whatever the majority voted for. He took no active part—broke no windows, unhorsed no mounted policeman, spoke at no meeting. Neither was he a "scab." As far back as 1900, long before the I.T.G.W.U. was organised, before Connolly wrote, or Larkin spoke to the Dublin dockers, Matt Talbot went on strike with a group of men at the Port and Docks Board, men who considered that they had just cause for striking. When the strike petered out, and the men slunk miserably back to work, in ones and twos at first, then in larger groups—only four men did not return, Dolan, McAuley, O'Reilly and Matt Talbot. The latter, who consulted a priest about the justice of the 1913 strike before he walked out, in all probability consulted his confessor, or some other priest, before going on strike in 1900. In 1913 he obeyed his Union when ordered to go back; in 1900 there was no proper organisation for casual workers like him; having gone on strike, he stayed on strike, though his fellow-workers gave up the struggle, and at a time when he had no Union to pay him strike benefit. He never went back to work for the Port and Docks Board after that.

His activity during the 1913 strike was not very spectacular, but it was none the less useful; out of his own scanty strike pay he contrived to spare money to fellow-workers, hard hit men whose children were threatened by hunger. Neither before nor after the strike—nor at any time—was he a man who curried favour with the "bosses." He told a friend that he spent the time of the strike praying and reading.

Present-day Trade Unionists give Matt his due. Senator Fintan Kennedy, General President of the I.T. & G.W.U., stated in a public address:

For Matt, virtue did not mean opting out. He was always prepared to face the consequences of full involvement. It is not presumptuous of us to regard him as a founder-member of the Trade Union movement.

The late lamented Senator Jimmy Dunne left his sick-bed to attend the unveiling of a commemorative plaque at 18 Upper Rutland Street, where Matt lived from 1903 to 1925. In the course of a moving tribute, the Senator said:

> Despite earlier detractions it has to be repeated that Matt Talbot was an early and respected member of the infant I.T. & G.W.U. and shared in the organising struggle of that courageous pioneer of Irish Trade Unionism. The Irish Trade Union movement, and particularly Matt's Union, is proud to be represented here today . . .He has left us an imperishable memory . . . . Today Dublin honours Matt Talbot; soon may Matt Talbot honour Dublin; then surely our city will have achieved its greatest glory and our workers their greatest leader.

A Derryman, Mr Stephen McGonagle, during his Presidency of the Irish Congress of Trade Unions, publicly stressed the same point:

> Matt was an involved Trade Unionist, one of the very first . . . one who stands out as a beacon light for Irish workers.

In June 1975 on the fiftieth anniversary of Matt's death, Father Morgan Costelloe, Vice-Postulator of Matt Talbot's Cause, addressed the annual Conference of the I.T. & G.W.U.

> Trade Unions are justly proud of members who distinguish themselves in politics, in business, or in industry, but your Union is unique. You have a former member who is a candidate for the Church's accolade of sainthood. If Rome decides to declare a new

workman-saint in the near future, it will be a great honour for Ireland, but it will be a particularly great honour for the I.T.G.W.U. You supported Matt Talbot when he was desperately poor in 1913 and again in 1923-24. He deserves your support yet again and, since you supported many good causes in the past, I appeal to you to officially support his Cause on this, the Golden Jubilee of his death.

Father Costelloe's appeal was not made in vain. At the conclusion of the Conference the delegates sent the following telegram to the Holy See:

> On the occasion of the annual Conference of the Irish Transport and General Workers' Union, and on behalf of 400 delegates representing 150,000 members, we respectfully request the Holy See to expedite the beatification of our former member, the Servant of God, Matt Talbot.

In the heat of the 1913 dispute both sides lost sight of the fundamental evil that was bringing Dublin—with both her workers and her employers—to the edge of doom. For the problem of too many hands for too little work had its roots in generations of misgovernment. The great disparity in Ireland's capital was not between the Irish employers and the Irish workers, but between the Irish of all classes and the armies of alien officials, place-hunters, top-heavy garrisons, and the hordes of hangers-on, high and low, who battened on the populace. All of these must have viewed with deep satisfaction the sharp cleavage caused in Dublin by the 1913 dispute. Those in authority decided that the dispute would have to be settled by outsiders, the Irish being assumed to be incompetent, altogether incapable of managing their own affairs. The issue became confused; Matt Talbot was not the only man who did not understand the matter, but few were humble enough to admit—even to themselves—that they did not know.

While the city was still trying to recover from the effects of the strike, the 1914 War broke out. At last there was work in plenty for the unemployed; the enlisting officers were busy. The rights and wrongs of small nations were being discussed everywhere; probably Martin's men were as vocal as any on the theme, "to 'list or not to 'list." The military bands played *It's a long way to Tipperary, Pack Up Your Troubles*, and—as the troopships moved past T. & C. Martin's yard out into Dublin Bay—*Come Back to Erin*.

Matt Talbot bought himself a few more books and pamphlets, including: *Catholicism and Peace; The Pope on Peace and War; Young Men of France and War; What is Orangism?; The Intellectual Claims of the Catholic Church; Life of St Columbanus* by Dr Myles Ronan; *Souperism; Memoirs of an Exiled Priest of '98*.

A nephew, one of the Andrews boys, newly 'listed in the British Army, called to see "Uncle Matt" on his first leave. His uncle told him he did not like to "see him in that uniform"; whereupon the nephew laughted heartily, but "Matt was not joking." He looked rather pale and tired, his nephew thought; it was a dull place, that room in Rutland Street, for a young "Tommy" home on furlough. He would not have gone to see Matt at all only his mother had insisted on it; the older man seemed to have no desire to hear of the life in the cross-Channel cities, nor of his nephew's experiences in France. The latter decided to cut the visit short; it was a very cold night and Matt had no fire. As the soldier took his departure, a sudden compassion for the silent little man who was his mother's brother moved him and, taking off the warm pullover—one of many knitted for the troops by patriotic English women—he forced it on Matt, wrung his hand and was away before the other could expostulate or refuse the gift.

That was in 1915—the year Matt's mother died. She was almost eighty. Since leaving Newcomen Avenue after 1895, she had lived successively at Upper Buckingham Street, Middle Gardiner Street, Gloucester Street, Henry Place and Hardwicke Street. In 1903, four years after her husband's death, Matt and herself had moved into the basement of 18 Upper Rutland Street. There she spent the last twelve years of her life. At the 1948 Enquiry her grand daughter told of how kind and devoted Matt was to his mother during those years. When she woke at night, she saw her son kneeling by his bedside praying. She was a woman of wisdom; she did not comment on his unusually long devotions; there is no record of her having gossiped to neighbours about Matt's doings. She told her daughters, but must have warned them about speaking of the matter outside, for her grand-daughter testified:

> We never spoke much about Matt outside our own family circle though we knew he was a holy man.

When his mother died, Matt was alone. But not lonely. To a lady who once complained to him of her loneliness after the departure of a favourite brother for abroad, he replied: "How can anyone be lonely, with Our Lord in the Blessed Sacrament?"

His nephew went back to the war: Matt Talbot continued, in the words of his foreman, Mr Carew, "doing as he thought right always." His prayer-books of this period contained small scraps of papers with headings of disaster: now the Allies lost, now the Germans: to Matt Talbot the numbers of fatal casualties were important in that it meant souls to be prayed for. Men for whom Christ died were being hurled into eternity—perhaps unprepared. Small nations, whose rights and wrongs were so much in the news at the outbreak of the war, were soon forgotten as the conflict gathered force; but in the light of the conflagration that lit Europe, one small nation began to see a way to right her ancient wrongs.

CHAPTER XI

TO SAY THAT MATT TALBOT TOOK NO
interest in politics is not to say that he took no interest in
his country's struggle for freedom. He never discussed
politics, his relatives stated, that was possibly because
Matt, knowing that one of the Andrew's boys was fighting
with the British Army in Flanders, thought that a
discussion of politics might cause dissention. Mr Paddy
Laird of Martin's, in an interview, stated that during the
years between 1916 and 1920, he frequently walked home
from work with his father and Matt Talbot; and the talk
often turned to the fight then in progress in Ireland. Matt
was a great admirer of the Jesuit preacher and
retreat-giver, Father Tom Murphy, who was frequently to
be heard in Gardiner Street, and who from 1917 onwards
was the Director of the Men's Sodality which met weekly
in the Jesuit Church there. Father Murphy was always
"Father Tom" to the men of his Sodality; he was a
magnificent preacher, capable of drawing and holding
vast congregations; faith, partiotism and old—almost
forgotten—traditions were the stops he played upon to
make his hearers remember their heritage, to encourage
them to recover and preserve it.

Mr Laird recalls that Matt often would say, "Were you
at Gardiner Street last night? Father Tom was great. It
would do you great to hear him." Men in the timber yard,
who had little inclination for sermons, but who were not
averse to hearing a pronouncement on the events then
stirring the capital and the whole country, would find

Matt Talbot near them at lunch-hour, or in the evening, telling them: "You should come up to Gardiner Street to-night (Sodality night); you'll be bound to hear Father Tom telling us something worth while."

Mr Michael McGuirk, already quoted, testified:

> Matt was a member of the Immaculate Conception Sodality in Gardiner Street Church and he recruited many members, including some "hard cases" for that Sodality.

Father Murphy's family could claim relationship with the famous Father John Murphy of the '98 Rebellion in Co. Wexford; so he was a man to whom partiotism was second nature. At this time, probably due to Father Murphy's influence, Matt Talbot began reading various Lives of the Irish Saints. Among his books there is one, *Lives of the Irish Saints*, also a short *Life of St Dymphna*, one of St Colmcille and another of St Patrick; there is also the *Life of St Columbanus*, written by Dr Myles Ronan for the 1915 Centenary.

It is interesting to note a few other pamphlets Matt acquired about this time. *The Plot, German or English?* and *The Case Against the Promised Boundary Commission* were published in 1918. Another pamphlet was entitled *The Nationalist Case Stated*. There was a newspaper cutting containing a brief sketch of Eamon de Valera, and others with brief accounts of Irishmen killed here and there throughout the country during the national fight. Matt evidently kept these to remind himself to pray for those killed; in some cases he had dates scribbled on the margins, probably a date on which he heard Mass or had Mass offered for the deceased. Or perhaps, as in the case of a certain Laurence Murray Doyle, a friend who died in 1899, the number in the margin denoted the length of time he meant to keep praying for the dead person. In Mr Doyle's case he wrote "April 1899, R.I.P. For two years."

Among Matt Talbot's books there is one magazine of which he had several copies, *The Catholic Bulletin*. Edited by the redoubtable "Sceilg"—the late J. J. O'Kelly—and published by Gills, the *Bulletin* came in for more than its share of attention from the British forces in the post-1916 period. One issue, having had some articles suppressed by the British Censors, appeared with blank pages as evidence of the suppression. Raids and battering rams were ordinary events in the *Bulletin's* existence. In the copies Matt had there was one with a detailed account of Lough Derg, then, as now, a centre of pilgrimage, penance and prayer. Matt had a leaflet of the pilgrimage and the prayers and programme of exercises in one of his books, suggesting that he himself had at some time gone to Lough Derg.

But the most thumbed-over copy of the *Bulletin* in Matt's possession was that of November 1916. The contents of that issue included slashing indictments of the "Irish Party" leaders, who had boasted in the Westminster Parliament of their offers to Kitchener at the outset of the 1914 war:

> We offered many thousands of Irish National Volunteers for home defence . . . Lord Kitchener said, "If you get me 5,000 men from Ireland, I will say thank you; if you say you will get me 12,000, I will say I am deeply obliged." . . . .

The main editorial demanded that before England set about restoring order in Ireland Dublin Castle should first be set in order. The Bishop of Cork, Dr Cohalan, in the course of a long article, commented on Leo XIII's Encyclical, *Rerum Novarum*. Matt Talbot was already familiar with this Papal Encyclical; he kept the *Bulletin* because one article carried names and photographs which were to him so many mortuary cards. Like Pearse's *Mother,* he would "speak their names to his own heart in the long nights."

These were the names Matt Talbot remembered:

GERALD KEOGH, aged twenty, pupil of Synge Street and St Enda's, member of the Holy Family Sodality, Rathmines. The son of a Fenian, he had served as one of the Fianna (the boys' organization affiliated to the Volunteers of 1916) before joining the Volunteers. On Easter Monday Padraig Pearse set him to Larkfield for a contingent of sixty men. On the way he stopped at Clarendon Street Carmelite Church for Confession; returning at dawn, he was shot dead outside Trinity College, receiving five wounds.

FRED RYAN, aged seventeen, not long left High Street National Schools; he had been a member of the Irish Citizen Army, and was in Liberty Hall day and night the week before the Rising. He was killed while bravely endeavouring to cover the retreat of his comrades at the corner of Harcourt Street and Stephen's Green on the Thursday of Easter Week. He was a member of the Sodality attached to St Audoen's Church, High Street.

PETER WILSON, aged forty, from Swords, who was detailed for service at Finglas on the Easter Monday, got confession on the nearby golf links on his way to take up duty. He was fighting under Captain Sean Heuston along the quays on the Tuesday morning, where he was killed. His mother was still (in November) making pathetic enquiries to know what had become of his remains.

JACK O'REILLY, a thirty-four year old Tralee man, a

technical instructor, who went early in life to New Zealand, where he took out degrees in Civil Engineering. He became principal of the Technical Schools in Tonga, capital of the Friendly Islands, and the King of Tonga each Christmas sent on to Ireland to "his beloved brother, O'Reilly," then principal of Ballinasloe Technical Schools and Technical Instructor for all Co. Galway, a wish—"live forever!" After the Rising he was arrested and imprisoned, first in Dublin, later in Frongoch; he was released in ruined health and died a few weeks afterwards of pernicious anaemia.

There was also a photograph of Roger Casement; and verses smuggled out of Frongoch to the Editor of the *Bulletin*. The last line of each verse was in Irish; but Matt must have made some efforts to learn the language—lessons from O'Growney and other phrase-lessons are in cuttings he evidently asked someone to save for him from a paper that was featuring a series of Irish lessons at the time.

Sir Joseph Glynn, relates that during Easter Week, 1916, Matt continued to attend Mass, heedless of the military cordons through which worshippers had to pass and which intimidated many.

Meeting a friend soon after, the latter questioned him on the subject of the Rising. Matt's reply was both shrewd and far-seeing. Referring to the executions of the leaders and the arrests and deportation which followed the insurrection, he said, "Our boys will all go into secret societies now . . ." In the Anglo-Irish war of 1919 to 1921 if anyone asked him had he heard of such and such a matter, he replied that he had not, as he did not read newspapers nor look at the placards. One morning the London and North Western Railway Hotel, then a British military centre adjoining Martin's yards, was blown up. The military immediately searched every place in the vicinity. It was just before the opening hour at Martin's—8 a.m.—and Matt Talbot, who was then working at the Castle Forbes yard, had arrived to open up. He was arrested in his little office, brought, with his hands up, across the yard to the entrance gate, placed against the wall and searched. He was then released. Later on, when he met Mrs Manning, who lived in the gate-lodge, he did not make any reference to his morning adventure, and when she tried to discuss the matter with him, he turned the conversation.

A newspaper report of the raid on the hotel runs as follows:

> At about a quarter to eight yesterday morning a determined bomb attack was made on the London and North Western Railway Hotel, North Wall, in which is billeted a force of about 100 Auxiliaries under the command of Major Ryan, and during the subsequent shooting by Auxiliaries and attackers the following casualties occurred. Killed: a man (name not given) stated to be one of the attackers. Wounded: Thomas Walsh, 19 Mark Street; James Shaw, 2 Ralph Place and Temporary Cadet Bodie.

Other reports stated that the Auxiliaries had been three weeks in occupation of the hotel; Major Ryan, the "Tan" officer in charge, stated in a Press interview that since they occupied the place "a rule had been made to keep the pavement clear, all pedestrians having to pass by in the roadway." The reason given for the occupation of the premises was "to superintend matters at the North Wall; to examine boats with a view to discovering ammunition, detecting suspects coming in, etc."

American sailors on the New York steamer *Honolulu* were witnesses of the firing and subsequent incidents. The attack lasted twenty minutes; all windows in the hotel were shattered by the explosion. "There was a wild stampede as over 100 dockers passing to work rushed for safety to the Railway Stores nearby." Half a day's work was lost; some of the Black and Tans fought in pyjamas; two dockers were hit by stray bullets; and, to add to the commotion, "the women-folk of the dockers ran to the place." A search among the dozen newspaper photographs taken that morning does not show Matt Talbot, a woman and child hurrying past the scene of the fighting being the only civilians to come within camera range.*

But the labour struggle, though it affected Matt closely as a worker, and the fight for freedom, though it must have stirred him as an Irishman and touched his life as a citizen of Dublin—the city that was the spearhead of the insurrection—made little or no impact on his inner life. All the time that interior life, silent and intense, expanded and grew; it surged strongly into every phase of the man's natural life, and Matt Talbot's ordinary human existence flowed into and mingled with this life within as the river with the sea.

In the last decade of his life, from 1915 to 1925, besides his spiritual reading and such reading as had a bearing on the industrial and national struggles, he read a good deal on controversial subjects; indeed, some of the titles of books and pamphlets he read when in his sixties, suggest that he had been asked questions either by persons who experienced religious doubts, or by non-Catholics, and was making sure of the correct answers. The books of this

* On the same day the newspapers carried photographs of queues filing reverently past the remains of Most Rev. Dr Walsh, Archbishop of Dublin, lying in state in the Pro-Cathedral.

period include: *Religion of the Hebrew Bible* (Hitchcock); *The Church in Scotland* (Rev. H. G. Graham); *Palm Sunday* (H. Thurston, S.J.); *Book, Bell and Candle: Exorcism and Anathema* (H. Thurston, S.J.); *Powers and Origin of the Soul* (Re. P.. M. Northcote); *Christian Science* (Herbert Thurston, S.J.); *The Church in Portugal* (C. Torrend, S.J.); *Some facts about Martin Luther* (Attenridge); *The Oath Against Modernism* (S. M. Smith, S.J.); *Jesuit Obedience* (S. M. Smith, S.J.); *"Secret Instructions" of the Jesuits* (John Gerrard, S.J.); *What the World Owes to the Papacy* (Monsignor Grosch); *The Blessed Sacrament, the Centre of Immutable Truth* (Cardinal Manning); *The Intellectual Claims of the Catholic Church* (Sir Bertram Windle, K.S.C.); *Will Any Religion Do?* (by a Benedictine writer).

Most of these were pamphlets, but there were other larger books, such as: *Thoughts in Time,* by Monsignor Ward; *Essays on Miracles,* by Cardinal Newman; *Christ Among Men;* a translation from Sertillanges (in this book Matt had marked the section headed "Jesus and Nature"); *St Paul and his Missions,* by Fouard; also two smaller books on St Paul; *St Leo the Great and the Dogma of the Incarnation; Mixed Marriage,* by the Bishop of Leeds; *Question Box of the Paulist Fathers,* by Father Bertrand Conway. In the latter book the Servant of God had marked the following questions, with their answers:

> Must Catholics believe that the world was created in six days?
>
> Why does the God of Truth permit so many false religious?

The Crucifix, the Most Wonderful Book in the World, by the Rev. Wm McLoughlin of Mount Melleray Abbey, was a spiritual book Matt Talbot seemed to use a good deal during his later years. He had, too, a little booklet entitled *The Providence of God,* compiled by Rev. Fr Murphy, the Director of his Sodality; he also had three books on devotion to the Holy Angels, and several prayers and leaflets in connection with St Michael, the Archangel, to whom he seemed to have special devotion. Lives of St Catherine of Siena, St Bridget of Sweden, St Elizabeth of Hungary, Venerable Oliver Plunket, now St Oliver Plunket, Blessed Peter Canisius, S.J., St Philip Neri; *A Life of St Teresa,* by Robert Kane, S.J.; a short Life of Cardinal Bellarmine by Aubrey Gwynn, S.J.: Lives of Suarez, Cardinal Newman, Père Lacordaire, etc., were among the books Matt read during his last years.

There were also the Lives of St Rita of Cascia, St Vincent Ferrer, Blessed M. Mary and Blessed Thomas More; the Addresses of the late Father T. Burke, O.P., and Addresses of Rev. Father R. Kane, S.J., on *The Evil of Drunkenness.* He had further books on Prayer and Meditation, bought about this time. *Elevation of the Soul to God,* by Robert Staples, O.C.D., had "R.I.P." inscribed in Matt's writing under the author's name. *The Science of the Soul;* Père Grou's *Meditations on the Love of God. Discourses on the Perfections and Wonderful Works of God* is a title indicating the direction his prayer had taken.

During all these years he was still visiting Clonliffe and Dr Hickey every Saturday. Occasionally—perhaps when Dr Hickey was away—he went to Father Walsh, S.J., in Gardiner Street, and in the last few years of his life he was often seen waiting outside Father "Tom" Murphy's confessional in the same Jesuit Church.

In his later years the churches he frequented

were—apart from the Jesuit Church of Gardiner Street, which was near where he lived—the Carmelite Church in Clarendon Street, the Franciscan Church in Merchants' Quay, the Dominican Church, Dominick Street, St Laurence O'Toole's, the Pro-Cathedral and St Joseph's, Berkeley Road.

The Fathers of Merchants Quay supplied the following statement to the 1948 Tribunal:

Matt Talbot was received into the Third Order (of St Francis) at the Franciscan Church, Merchants' Quay, Dublin, on October 12th, 1890, by Rev. Fr P. J. Cleary, O.F.M., and was admitted to profession by the same Father on October 18th, 1891. He was therefore, thirty-five years a member of the Third Order of St Francis.

His attendance was remarkable. In the first twenty years of his membership he was (according to the Register) absent only on *two* occasions from the monthly meetings—once in 1899 and once in 1909; he never seems to have been absent from the monthly Communion. From 1911 to 1916 he was absent from four meetings and was excused on one occasion. (On the last occasion he must have given some reason, probably illness, to some of the officials). In 1917 something unusual must have kept him from the monthly Communion from January to July and again from September to November. He must have attended the monthly meetings during that year, for he is marked "excused" only once—in November. In 1918 he was absent only once—in December—from both the monthly Communion and the monthly meeting. In 1918 the system of recording attendances was changed and it is not possible to give the exact number of his attendances for the seven years preceding his death. Still, it is pretty clear that he attended with the usual regularity during those years, for he was a well-known member at the meetings.

This attendance is all the more remarkable seeing that during his thirty-five years of membership he changed his address on six occasions, and at no period of his life was he in the immediate vicinity of Merchant's Quay.

Signed: Fr Cormac Daly, O.F.M., Guardian.

Mr Alwright, of Fade Street, who was for several decades a member of the choir in the Franciscan Church, recalls that on Sodality mornings Matt Talbot was always there before anyone else. On other Sundays, also, he frequently went on to that church for later Masses, the members of the choir being accustomed to point him out to one another as the "old reliable" who was always in the same place. Mr Alwright states that the reverent posture of Matt's motionless figure "drew your gaze like a magnet."

Rev. Father Lawrence, O.D.C., St Teresa's, Clarendon Street, wrote the following answer to a query made in May 1954:

Matt Talbot used to come very often to the 5.30 Mass in our church. The Brother Sacristan tells me that in or about 1924, Matt used to be waiting outside the church at 5 a.m., leaning against a pillar of the gate with a coat over his head. As soon as the Brother opened the church at 5 a.m., Matt used to come in and remain flat upon the ground for some minutes before the Blessed Sacrament before going to his seat.

I gave him Holy Communion often at the period referred to by the Brother. I only learned, years after his death, from Mr Woods (now deceased) who was President of our Vincent de Paul Conference, that the pious old man to whom I gave Holy Communion at the 5.30 Mass was Matt Talbot.

This was at a time when Matt had come out of hospital after spending two periods there. In 1924 Gardiner Street

Church did not open until after 6 a.m., first Mass beginning at 6.30. Yet people saw Matt back at Gardiner Street for the first Mass there; he must have heard the 5.30 Mass in st Teresa's and, after 6 a.m., hurried back to St Francis Xavier's. A fairly fast walker would cover the distance in anything from fifteen to twenty minutes.

The Superior of the Church of St Francis Xavier, Gardiner Street, Very Rev. Fr T. Mulcahy, S.J., supplied the following statement at the 1948 Enquiry:

> I have checked up on the facts concerning Matt Talbot's membership of the following Associations attached to St Francis Xavier's Church:
>
> Sodality of the Immaculate Conception and St Francis Xavier.
>
> Arch-Confraternity of Bona Mors.
>
> Pioneer Total Abstinence Association of the Sacred Heart.
>
> Apostleship of Prayer.
>
> None of the present Spiritual Directors was Director of his particular Association at the time of Matt Talbot's membership of it, but each has provided a written statement concerning the known facts of that membership from which I make the following summary:
>
> *Immaculate Conception Sodality:* No register of the Sodality kept before 1908. When the register was compiled that year, Matt Talbot's name was entered in it from the list of members of a particular Guild in the Sodality. There is no record of when he first joined this Sodality.
>
> *Arch-Confraternity of Bona Mors:* There is a written statement of one who was actually present when Matt enrolled—on some date during the 1914-18 War years. No pre-1918 register exists.
>
> *Pioneer Total Abstinence Association of the Sacred Heart:* The Pioneers have in their files a photograph of

Matt Talbot's actual membership card, with enrolment date in the Total Abstinence League of the Sacred Heart—the name used for the Association by Father Cullen before he formally established the Pioneers in 1898.

Apostleship of Prayer: Matt Talbot is registered as having been admitted on July 31st, 1917: there is a signed statement by the Promoter of the Apostleship who entered his name.

Matt Talbot was a regular attendant at the meetings of the above Associations until his death.

Signed: Timothy Mulcahy, S.J., Superior.
11th February, 1952.

Father Mulcahy enclosed a written, signed statement, made in March 1933, by Mr Patrick Breen, then President of the Immaculate Conception Sodality. He gave the same information regarding Matt's membership, but added that the usual subscription was 2d. a month. Matt Talbot always paid 1s. per month up to and on the day of his death. On the day he died (June 7th, 1925) he was present at Holy Communion and paid 1s. subscription.

Matt was also affiliated with some Sodalities in other countries. He belonged to a Confraternity of St Michael the Archangel; to St Joseph's Union, New York—Father Drumgoole's famous Orphanage Association; to a Crusade for the Preservation of the Holy Shrines in Palestine; to the Confraternity for the Agonising; to a similar Association with headquarters in Paris, the members of which undertook to spend an hour each month praying for the dying. He had acknowledgment cards from several Catholic charities, and was a regular subscriber to two foreign mission journals, *The Far East,* and the Holy Ghost Fathers' *Missionary Annals.*

As already mentioned, the Poor Clare Convent, Keady, Armagh, received regular alms from him. The Maynooth Mission to China, now known as the Columban Fathers, was the Missionary enterprise which appealed most to Matt and to which he constantly sent alms. St Columban's, Navan has the only letter from Matt Talbot that has been traced, and a transcript of which is given in the following chapter; it was received by them in December, 1924, six months before Matt's death.* Father Daniel Conneely, a former Editor of *The Far East,* made this written statement:

> The letter from Matt Talbot was undated, but our office stamp on it shows date of receipt and reads Dec. 31st, 1924. It was written on a page torn from a notebook.

> But Matt had been contributing to our Mission through a Mr William Kilbride of 72 Eccles Street, from December, 1920. On Dec. 7th, 1920, Mr Kilbride wrote:

> I enclose herewith Money Order for £4 towards the General Purposes of your Mission: £3 from Matthew Talbot and £1 from myself. As I am leaving town for some weeks on Monday please send acknowledgment to Talbot at 18 Upper Rutland Street and we don't wish our names to be published. And I would like, if you don't mind, to ask him to pray earnestly for your success. I know he does so, but still I think a request from you would come with greater force and I know no person, cleric or lay, whose prayers I would sooner have.

Mr Kilbride sent, in all, £37 on Matt Talbot's behalf to this Missionary society between December 1920 and June 1923. A letter in Irish, written by Mr Kilbride on June 5th, 1923, has this:

Abair paidir beag le h'aghaidh Talbóid atá i droch

---

* Cf. page 213

slainte. Tá sé ana-carthannach agus níl sé ach ina sclábhuidhe.*

The third, also in Irish, has this:

Tá feabhas mór ar Mhac Ui Talbóid ach ní féidir leis aon obair a dheanamh fós.†

Mr Kilbride's letters refer to the time Matt Talbot was ill in 1923, a year in which he spent two periods in the Mater Hospital. The late Professor Henry Moore, Senior Physician at the Mater, and Professor of Medicine at University College, Dublin, testified at the 1948 Enquiry that he first came to know Matt Talbot when the latter visited him before being admitted as a patient to the hospital in June 1923, or thereabouts. Dr Moore later knew him as a patient in the hospital. Having diagnosed that Matt was suffering from a kidney and heart condition, the doctor advised him to come into hospital for treatment; with great reluctance Matt allowed himself to be persuaded to do so:

> "I got the impression," stated Dr Moore, "that he was quite indifferent to his ailment and was prepared to accept whatever it pleased God to send him."

Matt Talbot was in the Mater from June 19th to July 17th, 1923, and from September 10th to October 27th of the same year.

> He behaved wonderfully as a patient, (continues Dr Moore's evidence) and in a saintly manner. He was an extraordinarily religious man. It occurred to me first that he might be a religious crank. I gathered that he gave away a good deal of his money to others, and I had the impression that he left himself short of food. He also told

---

*Say a little prayer for Talbot who is in bad health. He is very charitable, although only a labouring man.

† Mr Talbot is greatly improved but is unable to do any work yet.

me that he got up to go—fasting—to an early Mass (5 o'clock, I think). He told me, too, that he remained in the church for several Masses. I was not long in changing my opinion of him; I was very much impressed by him. He was one of the gentlest men I have ever come across, and were it not that I was so busy at that time I would like to have had him as a friend.

I wish to state that it was with reluctance on his part I was able to glean the above information about his life and austerities. I remember advising him to have something to eat after one Mass before going out to hear other Masses. I am fairly certain that he came back to me after his discharge from hospital, but I do not know how often he visited me nor when his last visit was paid me.

In answer to a query from the Rev. Judges, Dr Moore stated that the disease from which Matt Talbot suffered, while not painful in the ordinary sense, would give rise to a good deal of discomfort; in Matt's case it would have caused shortness of breath if he hurried or climbed stairs, and difficulty in breathing would make it difficult for him to sleep. Dr Moore did not think that Matt looked well, but neither did he look emaciated; the Doctor said that his illness could account for the latter fact, bodies of patients so affected being inclined to store fluid. The Doctor stated that Matt was a most obedient and submissive patient.

"Of all the persons I have met," the witness said in conclusion, "Matt Talbot seemed to me to be an outstandingly holy man."

Sister Mary Veronica Frost and Sister Mary Emmanuel O'Connor, nursing Sisters of Mercy in the Mater Misericordiae Hospital, also gave evidence. When Matt Talbot was first admitted to hospital on June 19th, 1923, he was in St Lawrence's Ward, then under Sister Veronica's charge; on July 2nd he was transferred to St

Brendan's Ward where Sister Emmanuel was in charge. The sisters were able to produce the hospital charts recording Matt's stay in the Mater. He must have been fairly ill when admitted, as two days after arriving he received the Last Sacraments; Sister Veronica's recollection of her patient is that he spoke hardly to anyone, except to a Mr MacDonnell, since dead. He was never able to be up.

When he was transferred to Sister Emmanuel's Ward, it was found that his pulse was abnormally rapid (160 per minute). He was allowed up but ordered to rest during the day on a couch in the hospital corridor. The Sister remembers him lying with his face to the wall; she had the impression that he was praying and that he was not interested in what went on around him. He was very silent; Sister noticed him saying his Rosary and visiting the Blessed Sacrament; when he was able to walk a little, the Sister saw that he held his beads in his hands walking about, but in such a way that it was hard for others to see the rosary; Sister would not notice this, she stated, only that she used to go looking for him in the grounds to ensure that he did not stay out too long. In the afternoons he went up in the lift to the chapel; he had been forbidden to kneel and Sister Emmanuel remembers him sitting in the back bench. He said nothing about his spiritual life; indeed, he hardly spoke at all.

The witness stated that Matt must have asked special permission to go up in the lift in the afternoons to the church as heart patients were always kept under special observation. Sister Emmanuel had a nickname for Matt. She called him "Poor old Tach," from his ailment, tachycardia. In an interview, the Sister also recalled how on one occasion a younger Sister was studying for an examination and remarked to her that she could not remember the anatomical structure of the sternum and chest cavity. Sister Emmanuel told her to go and examine "poor Tach"—that his ribs and breastbone were easily studied, "For of all the patients I ever saw," Sister added, "Matt Talbot is the one least covered with flesh."

Sister Veronica stated in evidence that when Matt returned to hospital in September he was under her care. When able to be up he used to spend much time in the organ gallery of the chapel:

> ....and he used to forget to come for his meals, and we used to have to send the nurse for him. On one occasion, I warned him that if he did not come at the proper time, I would give him a cold dinner. His answer was: "Sister, we must feed the soul as well as the body." He said this with a smile . . . . Later, after his death, when enquiries were being made about him, I asked Mr McDonnell, who was a diabetic and used to return periodically to the hospital, if he thought that Talbot, who had been a patient in the bed opposite him, was an exceptionally holy man. He said that he certainly was; he had seen him praying during the night, with arms outstretched and holding his rosary in his hand. He used to lead in the recitation of the Rosary in the Ward. He was very grateful for anything done for him; his disease could cause considerable suffering when he got the attacks. Matt did not complain. As far as I know, he ate whatever he got. I remember that he wore old clothes but they were clean. He wore a swallow-tail coat. A Mr Watt used to visit Matt in hospital; he was a great friend of Matt's and knew him intimately. He came to see me sometimes after Matt's death; he regarded him as a very holy man.
>
> As far as I can recall, Matt spent all his free time—from 11 a.m. to 1 p.m., and from 2 p.m. to 6 p.m.—visiting the Blessed Sacrament.He would have received Holy

Communion once a fortnight while in hospital, like other patients in that ward.

Sister Dolores McDermott also gave evidence:

I was Sister in charge of St Laurence's Ward when Matt Talbot returned there (Autumn, 1923). He was suffering from heart disease and was put to bed at once. He remained in bed nearly all the time he was in hospital. He did not then wear chains. He was very quiet and retiring and had little to say to anyone. He had a very sweet smile and was always very gracious in his manner. He took whatever food was given him, and made no comment or complaint. It was noticed that he did not use butter. His sister and a friend brought him eggs and fruit. These he handed to me without any remark . . .I gave them to him with his meals. He got very ill and I had him anointed. I sent for his sisters and told them he was dying, and said that it was as well he should die then, he was so well prepared. He seemed to be dying as he was scarcely breathing after having received the Last Sacraments. I now think he may have been in a state of profound recollection. His extraordinary calmness at the time struck me as remarkable. I said all the prayers for the dying. He got over this attack and two days later was able to go downstairs to have a cardiograph taken. He then returned to bed and after a few days more was allowed up.

The first day he was allowed up he disappeared and could not be found in the hospital or in the grounds. I thought he had gone out and had got an attack in the street. He was eventually discovered in a corner of the chapel, praying. When I complained to him that he had given all of us a great fright, he replied with his usual quiet smile, "I have thanked the nurses and the doctors, and I thought it only right to thank the Great Healer." These words made such an impression on me that I have since told the patients to go to the chapel to thank God for their recovery. At the various times he was in the hospital, the

Sisters noticed his great recollection in the chapel and observed that he never used a prayerbook. He was in the chapel every evening when the Sisters recited the Office. He was always to be seen in a remote corner kneeling quite erect.

He never asked for any privileges. He received Holy Communion every Monday. On other mornings, if any patient was to receive Holy Communion, I asked him if he would like to receive also. He always said "Yes" but he never asked for It himself. He did not speak of religious matters with the nuns. Some patients like to discuss religion, but Matt Talbot never showed by his conduct that he was anything more than a sweet-natured, holy old man. Knowing now the life of austerity which he led, it is obvious to me that he sought to conceal his holiness from all around him.

On October 27th, 1923, Matt Talbot was discharged from hospital. He was unable to work, and for some time had to visit the hospital dispensary regularly. As he was a member of the Builders Labourers' section of the I.T.G.W.U. he drew National Health Insurance from June 4th to November 26th, i.e., twenty-six weeks' benefit at 15s. a week. After that he was only entitled to draw a disability benefit of 7s. 6d. a week.

At the 1931 Enquiry, Mr Raphael O'Callaghan, giving evidence regarding this period of Matt Talbot's life, said that he (Mr O'Callaghan) secured a grant of £3 from the Society of St Vincent de Paul for his friend. When he visited him in hospital, Matt remarked, "Oh, I suffered." Later, when he heard of Matt's discharge from hospital, Mr O'Callaghan visited him in his room.

> I did pity him. He seemed very ill and destitute; he looked down and out. I suggested to him to go to the Little

Sisters of the Poor. He said the would rather be by himself; he added that he was shy.

Mrs Halbert stated that Matt had told her during the last months of his life that he suffered much from pain in his heart and that he used to get weaknesses.

There were some Vincent de Paul leaflets in his books for 1924, when he was probably being assisted by that Society. Some friends, Mr Ralph O'Callaghan and others, with great difficulty persuaded him to accept gifts of money at this period. But most of the time, from November 1923 until March 1925 he was very badly off; his illness and frequent lack of money began to tell heavily on him and to the man climbing life's mountain, time was paying out the last months, weeks, days and hours. The final stretch called for stiff endurance, but the climber had trained well; suffering, inactivity, a complete severance of the last few strands that bound him, awaited him at the end.

In January 1925 his friend, his counsellor, his Father in God died suddenly. Dr Hickey had been changed to St Mary's, Haddington Road, some months previously. He was in his middle fifties when changed from Clonliffe College to Haddington Road parish, and was now Monsignor Hickey. He was in his church on January 19th and was dead on the 20th. His death, though it would have stunned Matt Talbot, was perhaps not so hard to bear as an earlier trial: that parting had been preceded by an earlier one when Dr Hickey left Clonliffe. For, though Dr Hickey still kept in touch with Matt, it was not the same.

The regular Saturday evening Confessions in Clonliffe were no more; the little visits of Dr Hickey, made so often during those thirty years, were now of the past. Matt would have remembered how the young priest sought him out in Middle Gardiner Street, and in Gloucester Street, and Henry Place and Hardwicke Street; he would have recalled Dr Hickey's visits to Rutland Street, visits that were more frequent since Mrs Talbot's death in 1915—the talks about spiritual matters, the advice, the hymns they sang together, the big heart and kindly understanding of the man to whom, as to no one else in this world, Matt might unburden himself. If Matt Talbot ever wept, it was surely when Dr Hickey was changed to Haddington Road. He would hardly have grieved to hear of his friend's death for—to holy people—death is a matter more for joy than tears.

CHAPTER XII

FROM THE AUTUMN OF 1923 UNTIL THE SPRING
of 1925, when he went back to work, Matt Talbot was a
very poor man. Out of the reduced National Health
Benefit of 7s. 6d. a week he paid the rent of his room; the
remainder left him sixpence a day to live on. That amount
would probably have sufficed for his needs, long since
pared to the minimum; but it would not have permitted
him to continue his alms. He could no longer help the
Missions, or the Poor Clares of Keady, or Father
Drumgoole's orphans in New York; acquaintances down
on their luck, neighbours out of work, could count no
more on Matt for a helping hand. His health was gone and
he—a man of great natural energy—had to accept the
inactivity and consequent feeling of uselessness his
impaired physical condition imposed upon him. Gone,
too, was his livelihood, and with it his sense of security and
capacity, limited though it was, for helping others
materially. His friend, Dr Hickey, was gone; no other
could adequately take his place.

During the year that was to be his last Matt was called
upon to practise the uttermost degrees of detachment. In
his reading he would have learned that complete
liberation of the heart and spirit is no easy achievement;
everyone has something, small or great, exterior or
interior, to which he is attached. "For every man hath
purpose and desire, such as it is." The command, "Leave
all and follow me" implies renunciations so far-reaching
and so drastic as to dismay even the bravest—the word

"all" ruling out reservations, demanding absolute surrender. Beyond the barriers where some discard part of what most men deem indispensable lie further, more formidable, barricades; to scale these, eager souls divest themselves of all that still encumbers; while the intrepid few intent on overtaking the Christ whom they follow find the last stages of the road making yet greater demands on them; there they must rid themselves of attachment even to things seemingly good—one's way of helping others, of attaining perfection, of seeking God.

In December, 1924, the Maynooth Mission to China received the following note:

> Matt Talbot have done no work for past 18 months. I have Been Sick and Given over by Priest and Docter. I dont think I will work any more there one Pound From me and ten shillings From my Sister.

This donation was the last of Matt's little savings. Mrs Fylan told Sir Joseph Glynn that, when working, Matt had been accustomed to leave a little money in her care "for emergencies." During his illness, some of his friends had insisted on Matt's accepting gifts of money from them; this, too, he gave to Mrs Fylan. The ten-shilling donation to the Missions, mentioned in the letter as being given by Mrs Fylan, was sent by Matt as a little gesture of gratitude to his sister for having looked after him during his illness.

When the days lengthened and Matt felt a bit stronger he decided to look for work again—light work—anything rather than being idle. Brother Furlong, S.J. told the Tribunal:

> Some time after he came out of hospital, I met him in the church about mid-day one day. I went over to him and asked him how he was. He said "Just middling; but sure

it's the Will of God. I'm tired of being idle and knocking around. I'll go back to work again."

Shortly afterwards the Brother heard from a man who knew Matt that the latter had gone back to work in T. & C. Martin's. Mrs Johnson's evidence on the same point was that her uncle was unable to work for some time after coming out of hospital, but that eventually he went back to Martin's and was working there up to the very day before his death. Mr Carew, the foreman under whom Matt Talbot worked, affirmed this and added that, when he resumed work with the firm, his daily round was less arduous as the other workmen left the lighter tasks to Matt.

Mrs Donnellan of 18 Rutland Street recalled an incident in connection with Matt's illness. Before he was removed to hospital, Mrs Donnellan's husband, Francis Donnellan, and her son Jack often went up to visit Matt in his room. One night Jack Donnellan thought that their neighbour seemed much worse than usual and he offered to sit up with him for the night; but Matt would not hear of it; he said that it would be unjust to deprive the young man of his sleep, as he had to work next day; and he added "Nobody can keep me if Our Lord wants me."

When he returned to work after his illness and two periods in hospital, he led, Mr and Mrs Donnellan stated, the same austere life as always. The only concession he made to his debility was that on Sundays, instead of fasting from early morning until after the last Mass, he returned to the house after the earlier Masses and took a little breakfast—usually a cup of shell cocoa—before going out to other Masses. Mr Donnellan was often on night work and had to sleep during the day; the family seldom heard Matt entering or leaving the house and concluded that he walked noiselessly up and down the stairs out of consideration for the man who was trying to sleep.

When Matt Talbot first went to live in Rutland Street, he and his mother were in the basement flat, and his fellow-tenants often heard him singing hymns in the evenings or at night—so much so that some of them expostulated with him. When the top flat became vacant he moved up there; after that he was seldom heard singing, but possible explanations for this could be that sound travels up and that his neighbours had by this time become so used to hearing him that they no longer noticed. Once, a woman awake all night attending to a sick child heard someone singing hymns at two in the morning; she had some difficulty in calming down her sister who had come to keep her company in her vigil and who was very alarmed on hearing the voice from the attic. The witness said "I told her it was only Mr Talbot." Several witnesses stated that Matt was a very sweet singer.

If he looked out of his little window he could have seen, not five minutes' walk from his attic room, the grey walls and green fields of Clonliffe, a place dear above others to Matt Talbot; but from the evidence of those who knew him best there does not emerge a man who had time for such luxuries as gazing out of windows or remembering the happiest days of his life. Rather does it suggest that the reason Matt Talbot paid more than half of his 7s. 6d. a week in the winter of 1924-25 to keep his room was to ensure solitude; through the windows of his soul entrancing vistas stretched their limitless distances; there was no need for remembrance—the best was yet to be.

Dr Moore warned Matt when he left hospital in 1923 that he might die suddenly of heart disease at any time. When Mrs Fylan heard this she urged her brother to carry in his pocket a piece of paper indicating his name and address, in case of an accident. But Matt replied "What do I need with my name and address? Won't God be with me when I die?"

Matt met Ted Fuller soon after he was discharged from hospital and told him that his heart was affected and he doubted that he would ever be able to work again. Later on, Mr Fuller heard that Matt was returning to T. & C. Martin's. When he went back to work, two men were sent to help him in the yard, as he was still very weak. He was not able for work but he kept on. Mr Manning stated that Matt resumed the work he had always been doing, but he could regulate the load of timber he had to lift and so ensure that he would not overtax his strength. Mrs Manning met Matt at Martin's gate the day he came back to work. He said he came "to speak to Mr Kelly"—one of the principals of the firm—and told Mrs Manning that he was very anxious to get to work again. He was working at Martin's every day from that until the day before his death.

He was almost sixty-nine. More than four decades of prayer and rigorous penance stood between the Matt Talbot of 1884 and the ageing workman of 1925. During all those years he passed for an ordinary labourer, dependable beyond the ordinary, unusually careful and conscientious about his work, more silent and self-effacing than his fellows. A few knew him to be a man of constant prayer, one who denied his body food and ease and comfort; hardly any knew of his nightly vigils, of his few hours' repose on a plank bed and wooden pillow; no one was allowed to see the chains that bound his body and limbs in such fashion that with every movement some portion of his frame suffered constriction, if not actual pain. Probably no one but his confessor knew the whole story of God's dealings with the Dublin workingman, Matt Talbot, and of the latter's interior life—"hidden with Christ in God."

More than once he tried to induce others to take up some spiritual practice which he himself had found helpful. He told one "What I can do, surely you can." To another he remarked "It's constancy God wants." He himself had been constant and God had given him right royal rewards. Once, he confided to a friend that the hardest thing in his whole life had been the keeping of the pledge for the three months when he first took it in 1884. Perhaps it was his fidelity in that one matter which earned for him the grace to be faithful in harder tests. It seemed a small thing, but it was no easy effort for the young man, Matt Talbot, to take and keep the resolution which conquered the vice that stood between him and God.

As self-indulgence had been his downfall, so self-denial was the ladder by which he climbed to holiness. Beginning with that three-month pledge against drink which he took from Dr Keane in Clonliffe College in 1884, he overcame in a very short time the habits of intemperance which had for sixteen years enslaved him. After the three months he took a pledge for a longer period; within a year of his conversion he took it for life. A few years later he was one of the first to enrol in the newly-formed Temperance Association of the Sacred Heart. He was Number 133 on the Register of what later became known as the Pioneer

Association.* Matt's three-month pledge of 1884 had become for him not merely a life-pledge but an instrument of atonement for the excesses of so many—excesses which he himself had known only too well.

Ireland in 1925, though still suffering from the effects of the Civil War that followed on the departure of the British, was a vastly different country from the Ireland of the previous generation. Green pillar-boxes and green post-vans had replaced the red; the khaki uniforms had vanished from the streets of the capital and the chief garrison towns, and the citizens gradually became accustomed to the green-clad National Army. The "black and Tans" were but a nightmare memory; instead of the black jackets of the "peelers," the navy-blue of the Civic Guards became a familiar sight as the new police force directed traffic. The days of depression were done. "Winter was over and past and spring had appeared in our land." There were motors and buses everywhere and the occasional excitement of an aeroplane overhead.

Matt Talbot continued his vigils, his fasts, his prayers, his work. He was re-reading two books, Newman's *Essays on Miracles*, and the translation of a treatise, *The Pearl among the Virtues: Chastity*. In the one he left as marker a leaflet with the dates and titles of the Lenten Lectures being preached in Gardiner Street that Lent by Father George Byrne, S.J. In the other was a leaflet commemorating the preaching of the Three Hours Agony on Good Friday 1925. Easter gave way to Ascension, and Pentecost came and went. The heat-wave that had

* The Pioneer movement was founded by Fr James Cullen, S.J., in 1899. Its members, all volunteers, take a life pledge against alcohol and pray daily for the conversion of drink addicts. Their commitment has a spiritual motivation.

parched both Europe and America in May 1925 reached Dublin during Whitsuntide. Whit Sunday, May 31st, and the Bank Holiday were exceptionally cold, with showers of hail and rain. But by mid-week Dubliners were sweltering under a broiling sun. Temperatures ranged from almost 70 in the shade to 80's in the sun. The barometer soared. Trinity Sunday dawned in a haze of heat.

The hospitals were kept busy and city ambulances were in constant demand. A woman who had been rescued from the canal at Charlemont Mall was taken to Jervis Street Hospital on the Saturday night. Next morning she was little the worse of her experience. By then Jervis Street Hospital had had further ambulance arrivals, among them an able seaman of the *SS. Killarney,* who had collapsed and died while unloading heavy cargo. Heart-failure, the intern said—not the injuries received when the deceased man fell beneath his load.

On Trinity Sunday, June 7th, Matt Talbot set off early, intent on completing his usual Sunday morning programme of prayers and Masses. A month had passed since his sixty-ninth birthday; for forty-one years he had been trudging the rugged paths of penance, climbing the peaks of prayer. Age was beginning to tell on him. In obedience to Dr Moore he had made slight modifications in his time-table on Sundays; it was no longer a question of attending as many Masses as possible; much though he would have liked to do so he refrained, knowing that in God's sight the submission of one's will to lawful authority is a greater good than sacrifice.

In former days he used to attend with his Sodality in Gardiner Street on the first Sundays of each month; on second Sundays he would be in Merchant's Quay for the monthly Communion of the Third Order Brothers; and afterwards he would go on at once to other churches, mostly to the Pro-Cathedral, his own parish church, the mother-church of the Archdiocese where he had been baptised. There one could be sure of many Masses, as clergy passing through Dublin stayed at one or other of the hotels in the vicinity. In a little book entitled *The End of the Society of Jesus,* where he had marked the section on Chastity and Obedience, he had written in a margin "August 29th, Feast Seven Joys Virgin Mother, 1909, 19 Masses." He made a mistake in the date as the Feast mentioned was then held on August 22nd, but he celebrated the Joys of Our Blessed Lady in good measure in 1909 as in other years; in an old prayerbook there was a note dated Sunday, August 15th, 1915, when he attended twenty-one Masses, and overleaf in the same book he wrote "On the Feast of the Seven Joys, B.V.M., August 22nd, 1915, I, Matt Talbot, was present at twenty-one Masses."

Perhaps on the Trinity Sunday morning of 1925 his mind went back to these and other red-letter days marked in his well-worn prayerbooks and in the spiritual books he read. There was the Solemn Inauguration of the Month of the Sacred Heart in Gardiner Street Church in 1910; it had been a great occasion and for these days Matt meditated on the 12th and 13th Stations of the Cross—the Crucifixion and the Taking Down from the Cross. It should have been particularly easy for him to meditate upon the Taking Down from the Cross as he habitually knelt at the end of a pew, three seats from St Joseph's altar—in a position where he could also see the high altar and another side altar—and directly in front of the 13th Station.

There is no clue to the note "Memento of May 31st, 1896"; nor any indication why he was moved to write "Lord, thou hast been our refuge always" in a margin, underneath which he added "June 25th, 1892, Feast of the Sacred Heart." "September 12th, 1909," was noted in a book entitled *Conditions of Prayer;* "June 1910," was inscribed over an article on perseverance in virtue. He had marked one of his favourite authors, Bishop Hedley, at passages on perseverence, the grace of graces which the Benedictine advised his readers to pray for daily. "Our life consists," wrote Dr Hedley, "of days, and each day has to be lived through in God's holy grace and in increasing nearness to Him . . . The work requires an enlightened spiritual sense and manly resolution . . . Let us, with all our fervour, pray daily for fidelity . . . Let us think of our falls . . . ." In 1922 Matt attended all Father Michael Garahy's Lenten Lectures in the Jesuit church on "The Idols of Society." These lectures made such an impression on him that he got the papers that reported them and kept the cuttings.

There is no reason to suppose that even had he received any premonition that Trinity Sunday, 1925, was to be a day of days for him he would have made any change in his usual Sunday morning routine. For to Matt it was not routine—the kneeling for long hours, the renewal of Calvary each time Mass succeeded Mass—for him prayer and penance were but the silent fountain-heads of joy and peace. His fellow tenants in 18 Rutland Street did not hear him go out that morning; but they hardly ever heard him go out or come in. People whose work took them abroad early—Gardai, milkmen, paper-sellers, those who were returning from night-work—had become so used to seeing his bowed figure outside St Francis Xavier's long before the church opened each morning, that afterwards no one could remember whether he had been there that morning or not. Passers-by had long ceased to comment on the little man kneeling outside the church or, if a crowd were there, further down the street on the steps of the convent of the Irish Sisters of Charity. Morning after morning he was there, his muffler knotted round his throat, his bowler hat beside him on the ground. To a few still living in that area of Dublin he was as familiar a sight at the four columns that front the spacious church crowning the summit of Gardiner Street—that long, arterial roadway which climbs from where the Custom House skirts the Liffey to the northern rim of central Dublin.

Mr Laird, interviewed concerning that morning, said that Matt used to kneel near him at Soldality meetings. He remembered that Sunday well when, two days later, Matt was being spoken of by the men in Martin's. He recalled that when the men stood up to sing a hymn to Our Blessed Lady, Matt stood up and sang with the rest; but when the singing was over and all knelt down Matt forgot to kneel and remained standing, seemingly oblivious of everything and everyone, until someone near him nudged him. It was most unusual for Matt not to kneel when everyone else knelt; he was always eager to resume his intent concentration on the altar and what was happening there.

The books of the Immaculate Conception Sodality show that Matt was present at the monthly Communion that morning and paid his usual shilling-a-month subscription. It is likely that he had been in the church from 6 a.m. or earlier. Mr Mulvanny, a fellow-tenant of 18 Rutland Street, met him in the hallway sometime before 9 a.m. It was another scorching day. Thinking that Matt looked poorly, and remembering that he had been in hospital for two periods during 1923, his neighbour advised him to rest. Matt told him that he felt a bit weak. It is likely that he had been fasting strictly on Saturday, June 6th, as on the previous Wednesday and Friday—those three days being Ember Days. Then he went up to his room on the top floor. Possibly he drank a little of the cold-tea-and-cocoa mixture that was his only beverage. Half an hour later he was out again. Mr Mulvanny spoke to him as he went out. In a statement made and signed before his death in St Kevin's Hospital in 1936, John Mulvanny said:

> When he came downstairs again he looked weak. I remarked to him that he should not go out until he had rested himself. He was smiling and said that he felt all right and that he was going to Dominick Street Church. I waited at the door until he went round the corner into Great Charles Street . . . That was the last I saw of him alive. I was going to follow him but as I knew he was a man who did not wish anyone to "pass remarks" on him, I went on instead to Gardiner Street.

Though the morning was very warm, the Servant of God was probably hurrying as he made his way to St Saviour's, the Dominican church. Patrick Farrell, who gave evidence at the 1931 Enquiry, and who had known Matt Talbot well for thirty years, stated "Matt could never get enough of the Holy Mass. You would meet him running to it." To get to Dominick Street he had to traverse two sides of Mountjoy Square and a fairly long street taking in Gardiner Place, North Great Denmark Street and Gardiner's Row; then he crossed the main north-south centre-city thoroughfare and passed along one side of Parnell Square. It was a heavenly morning. But to Matt

Talbot all mornings were heavenly. When men said, "Fine day, Matt," or "That's a changeable day, Matt," or "Bad day, Matt," he invariably answered "Every day God sends is good." Sunday, June 7th, 1925, was good. It was the Feast of the Holy and Blessed Trinity. Soon the priest in the Dominican church would read the *Introit:*

> Blessed be the Holy Trinity and undivided Unity: we will give glory to Him because He hath shown His mercy to us.

Turning into Granby Lane Matt stumbled, falling helplessly at the wall on the left-hand side. A few people noticed him and ran to his aid. Mr William Chambers who at that time lived in Parnell Square had been to the 9 a.m. Mass in Dominick Street that morning; he gives the following account of what happened:

> It was the Holy Communion morning for the Sodality of grocers' assistants and, being one of the prefects I marked the card for members and I would say that it was about 9.45 a.m. when I left the church to return home through Granby Lane.

> When I came as far as Mrs Keogh's shop, I saw a man lying on the roadside near the shop; two young men were holding up his head. (This shop was at the right-hand side of the lane; Matt Talbot had fallen at the opposite side and had been carried to the shop doorway.) Then I saw Mr O'Donohoe, who owned a public house nearby, coming out from Mass, and he went back for a priest. The late Father Walsh, O.P., came and attended to the dying man. There were about twenty people present and we all knelt down as Father Walsh said the prayers.

Writing in the *Universe* in 1948 a Mr W. J. O'Brien of Rugby described what happened in Granby Lane thus:

> Matt Talbot was walking less then five feet in front of

me. I saw him shudder, partly turn, and fall to the ground. I ran to him as also did a young man named Walsh. We loosened his shirt-collar but I knew he was dead. I ran to Dominick Street Priory and brought a priest. When the priest saw him he knew life had left him.

We knelt down and prayed for the repose of his soul.

Mr Noel Carroll of 32 St Alphonsus Road, Drumcondra, states in a letter:

My father was manager of a chemist's shop at Bolton Street. On every second Sunday he was on duty there and, before opening, would generally attend the 10 o'clock Mass in Dominick Street. On some Sundays he would take me along with him; I was with him on Sunday, June 7th, 1925. Though I was only eight and a half years at the time I remember that morning very well, as it was my first contact with death and made a deep impression on me.

It was a very sunny morning and as we turned into Granby Lane we noticed a lot of excitement centred around a man lying on the ground. My father, being a chemist, went over to render First Aid; I saw him opening the stud of the man's shirt collar. There was quite a crowd of people at this time and I remember my father telling them to stand back a bit. As they stood back I got a good look at the man to whom my father was attending. He had no collar or tie, and wore a grey suit; his eyelids were open and he appeared to stare. His face was round, not long and drawn, like some of the pictures that have been made of him. It was about 9.40, as the bell had begun to ring for the 10 o'clock Mass.

Two nurses returning from Mass in the Dominican church to the Nurses' Home in 34 Parnell Square were also on the scene. Nurse O'Leary gave evidence at both Enquiries. She said there were "seven or eight" present when she and her companion arrived on the scene; she went to the seemingly unconscious man, and finding him "pulseless," sent onlookers for the priest and doctor. She told them that Dr Eustace of Parnell Square was in the church. Some boys in the crowd ran round to Parnell Square and fetched Garda O'Hanlon; he rang for the ambulance. These three and others interviewed have a vivid recollection of the scene. Conspicuous in the hushed lane was the tall figure of the Dominican, Father Walsh, bowed down to render spiritual assistance to the still figure that was the cause of the commotion; draped upon the dust of Granby Lane, the cream and black of the Dominican robes looked like a flag—dipped in salute to death.

Sometime after 9.30 a.m. the Tara Street ambulance, unusually busy that week-end attending to heat-wave casualties, was 'phoned for again. Officer Rogers took the call and set off with three firemen and a driver for Granby Lane, at the back entrance to St Saviour's Church. A few people were there when they arrived, Mr Rogers says, among them the late Dr Eustace of Parnell Square, called from the church to attend the man who had collapsed in the laneway. Mrs Keogh, owner of the shop on the right-hand side of the lane, was there as was her son "Myler". She had seen the man stumble and fall and had called to her son; between them they had lifted the stricken man to their doorway. Dr Eustace wrote the following statement:

> I, Dr E. P. Eustace, attended Matthew Talbot on 7th June, 1925, when he died in Granby Lane on his way to the Dominican Priory Church. He died on the left side of the road about three feet from the path on way from Parnell Square. He died in my opinion from heart failure.

After the arrival of the ambulance the group that had gathered broke up, Father Reginald Walsh returned to the Priory; Dr Eustace hurried back to the church. Garda Hanlon asked if anyone present knew who the dead man was. Receiving no reply, the Garda went through the pockets of the grey suit; the search yielded a rosary beads and a prayerbook—nothing else; no name, no address, no clue as to the dead man's name or place of residence.

One of the Tara Street men lifted the bowler hat from the corner into which it had rolled when its wearer fell; his companions lifted the body into the ambulance. It was that of a fairly old man—a man of small stature and slight build. Charles Manners, mortuary attendant, and Laurence Thornton, porter, were on duty at Jervis Street Hospital when the ambulance arrived. Garda Hanlon had come along too, as was his duty. The Occurrence Book at Fitzgibbon Street Garda Station had a report entered by the then Station Sergeant, Timothy Maher, to the effect that while Garda Thomas Hanlon was on duty at Parnell Square some boys informed him that an old man was lying unconscious in Granby Lane. The police report continues:

> The Garda proceeded to the place immediately and saw the man lying on his back in the lane. The Corporation ambulance arrived soon afterwards and conveyed the man to Jervis Street Hospital where, on admission, life was pronounced extinct by Dr Hannigan, House Surgeon.
>
> Chris Keogh, 4 Granby Lane, stated that he saw the deceased walking down Granby Lane towards Dominick Street Church when he fell by Keogh's door. The man was not known in the locality and the Garda was unable to get any further particulars about him.

> Description: about 50 years, 5 feet 8 inches,* medium
> build, brown hair turning grey, nearly bald, grey
> moustache. He was wearing an old grey tweed suit,
> "Kildare House" on the tab, black hard hat, black laced
> boots, blue shirt with red and white stripes.

The suit was one which had been given him by Raphael
O'Callaghan. Although Matt was then almost seventy, the
Garda took Matt to be "about 50 years."

Meanwhile, in Jervis Street Hospital, the customary
routine was followed. A priest was 'phoned for and Father
McArdle of the Pro-Cathedral came immediately; it is not
certain whether he anointed the body of Matt Talbot or
not. The nun in charge of the Accident Ward, Sister M.
Ignatius, made the following statement to the Apostolic
Process:

> I was sent for when the remains arrived and when I
> entered the Accident Ward I think a nurse on duty told me
> that he (the dead man) had already been anointed by Fr
> Walsh, O.P. Father McArdle had been called in the
> meantime. He came but I am sure that he did not anoint
> the man, as we had been informed that he was already
> anointed.

The evidence of Charles Manners, mortuary attendant
at Jervis Street, Hospital, conflicted with that of the nun:

> The remains were brought to the hospital in a
> Corporation ambulance. A priest was 'phoned for; I
> remember the priest coming and anointing the dead man.
> I do not remember who the priest was.

Mr Manners and another attendant, Laurence
Thornton, undressed the dead man when the priest had

---

* Obviously an error. 5' 8" would be too tall. "Hardly five feet tall" was
the opinion of men who knew Matt. "Below middle height" was Mr
Raphael O'Callaghan's description of him.

gone. The found a chain "about the size of a horse's trace, the links being about half-an-inch long, wound round the body." On one arm was a lighter chain, on the other a cord. There was also a chain below one knee, immediately below the kneecap, "so placed that it must have caused pain when kneeling"; Charles Manners went for Sister M. Ignatius, and asked her to come and see what they had found. The Sister's evidence states:

> When I went down I saw the chains which were still binding the body. I remember distinctly the chain around his waist; I also noticed the cord and chain on his arms; the porters told me he had a chain on his leg.

The porters said that the chains were not imbedded in the flesh but that they had worn grooves on the skin and seemed to have been worn for a long time. All three commented on the spotlessly clean condition of the body and clothing. The Sister left instructions that the chains were to be removed from the body and to be put in the coffin with the remains after the inquest.

Nobody had any idea of who the dead man might be. The *Irish Independent* of June 8th carried the following paragraph:

UNKNOWN MAN'S DEATH

> An elderly man collapsed in Granby Lane yesterday, and on being taken to Jervis Street Hospital he was found to be dead. He was wearing a tweed suit, but there was nothing to identify who he was.

On the Sunday night Mrs Fylan, Matt's sister, came to Francis Donnellan of 18 Rutland Street in a great state of anxiety, saying "Matt is missing." Mr Donnellan went with her to Fitzgibbon Street Garda Station, explained the case, and the sergeant made some enquiries by telephone, but without result. This seems rather strange, seeing that there was an entry in the Occurrences Book for that Sunday concerning the accident case in Granby Lane. However, during the night the police evidently contacted Jervis St Hospital, for in the early hours of the morning a Garda called to Mrs Fylan to ask her to go to Jervis Street Hospital. She called to Mr Donnellan who again accompanied her. They saw the body of Matt Talbot, and the chains "lying on a small table nearby." When the Sister came in she asked Mrs Fylan "What are those chains?" Mrs Fylan said "Matt wore them when he was alive." When the Sister asked what should be done with them, Mrs Fylan said they were to be put in the coffin.

An inquest was held on Monday, June 8th, by the City Coroner, Dr Louis Byrne. On the Death Certificate the cause of death was given as Myocardial Degeneration.*

Although he died on Sunday June 7th, Matt Talbot was not buried until Thursday, June 11th, the feast of Corpus Christi. On the Wednesday evening his friend, Mr Raphael O'Callaghan, who "had not seen him since he went back to work a couple of months earlier, learned, accidentally, of his death." Mr O'Callaghan sent word to Father Flood, then in the Pro-Cathedral. That evening, for the last time, the Servant of God went into St Francis Xavier's. Among those who carried his remains into the church was his fellow-worker and friend, John Robbins. The coffin was placed in the Sacred Heart Chapel, and there, for the vigil of the Feast of the Blessed Sacrament,

---

*The City Coroner, Dr McErlean, confirms that an inquest was held. The Death Certificate also states that there was an inquest. The Dublin Cemeteries Committee's records likewise state "Burial on Coroner's order."

the dead man rested where so often the living man had worshipped.

Mr Laird, of Martin's, who was at Gardiner Street that evening, says that there were not many present. On the following morning the funeral left the Jesuit church after 11 a.m. Three men from T. & C. Martin's were there; so were Mr O'Callaghan, Father Flood, the Fylan and Andrews families, and several men belonging to the Sodality of the Immaculate Conception. The day being a Church holyday, there would have been many spectators; Dublin being a most sociable city, it is almost certain that already people were speaking of Matt Talbot; his austerities, for so long a secret shared with God alone, were no longer unknown. The obscure, "unskilled" labourer had for over forty years hidden his holiness; the suddenness of his end revealed things that Matt Talbot would have concealed had he got warning of death's approach.

The funeral went out the way so many Dublin funerals go, by the north-west road to Glasnevin Cemetery. The burial ground is on the site of the victory of the first English invader, Strongbow, over King Roderick O'Connor's army. Since the cemetery had been blessed by Dr Yore of Arran Quay in 1832, many a memorable funeral had taken the road to Glasnevin. Philpot Curran was buried there, and O'Connell the Liberator, and Mangan the poet; there lies Anne Devlin, so loyal to Emmet; and Hogan the gifted sculptor, and scholars like O'Donovan and O'Curry, and a long succession of holy and zealous priests, of selfless patriots, of noble and generous-hearted citizens whose passing had been a real bereavement to the poor of the city who sorrowfully saw their funerals pass by on the way to the cemetery.... Matt's was a poor man's funeral, the cost not exceeding £10.

After his death Matt Talbot's reputation for holiness became widespread. In 1931 the first enquiry into his life began and six years later a Papal Decree, introducing his Cause was signed. The second enquiry, part of the normal procedure towards beatification, began later and in 1949 forty witnesses were examined by the Tribunal set up to conduct investigations. In 1952 Matt's remains were exhumed and removed from the grave where he had been buried to a vault in the central circle of Glasnevin cemetery. One of those present had been an altar-boy in Berkeley Road church when Matt Talbot used to pray there; he was the President of Ireland, the late Sean T. O'Kelly. In February 1962 the remains were removed again, this time to the church of our Lady of Lourdes in Gloucester Street, the parish church of the area where Matt spent his life. The tomb of Wicklow granite has a glass panel in front showing the coffin. It bears a plaque inscribed THE SERVANT OF GOD, MATTHEW TALBOT. 1856-1925.

In that tomb, so dear to Dublin, Matt Talbot's remains await the final resurrection. People come to pray there, some in ones and twos, some in organised pilgrimages hundreds strong. They come not only from Dublin but from the most distant parts of our island, from England and Scotland, from Europe, from the farthest ends of the earth. They pray *to* Matt, remembering how his friend Dr Hickey asserted that he had never known Matt Talbot to ask God for a favour but it was granted. They pray for him, that he may yet be raised to the altars of the Church and honoured with the title of Saint. Saints are saints, however, not because of the official proclamation, but because they are holy, and the secret of Matt's attraction is holiness, for sanctity has a magnetism all its own. Standing before his tomb one wonders that a man almost unknown during his lifetime should have become famous in death, that an obscure, unskilled labourer should have acquired an influence extending far beyond the boundaries of Dublin, far beyond the shores of his native land. One recalls how, on the building schemes of a century ago, the foremen always put Matt first, to set the pace for other workers. It has pleased God, the Master-Builder, in the building of that city not made with hands, to raise up Matt Talbot—*pauper, servus et humilis,* poor, serving and lowly—and put him before us, to set the pace.

234

BIBLIOGRAPHY

Author's Note: This book, a revised edition of the original published by Gills in 1954, is based on the following sources:

1. The sworn evidence given by sixty-eight persons who knew Matt Talbot at the two Enquiries into his life and virtues. The first tribunal began its sittings in 1931, six years after Matt's death; the second Enquiry opened in 1948. Some witnesses gave evidence at both.

2. Personal interviews with fifty persons; some had given evidence at the second Enquiry, some at the first and second. Seven interviewees did not present themselves before the tribunals, thinking that what they had to relate would be considered unimportant and irrelevant. Pat Doyle, the octogenarian who had been Matt's boon companion before the latter's conversion, had not heard of the Enquiries.

3. Matt Talbot's books, notes etc., which are preserved at Archbishop's House, Dublin.

4. Files of daily newspapers 1850 to 1925.
   Files of the Irish Transport & General Workers' Union.
   Files of the *Dublin Historical Record* (organ of the Old
      Dublin Society).
   Files of *The Catholic Luminary, The Catholic Bulletin,*
      the *Far East* etc.
   Records of the Dublin Port & Docks Board.
   Records kept by the firm of T. & C. Martin Ltd (firm no
      longer extant).
   Records of the Christian Brothers.
   Records of the Pioneer Association.

Papers of the Holohan family.

Papers lent by Mr Birney of the Transport & Science Museum Society.

Catholic Directories for the 1850 to 1925 period.

Post Office Directories

Thoms' Directories

Registers of several city churches.

Besides the above primary sources, a number of works bearing on the religious, social, political and economic history of Matt's time were used, principally those listed below;

Augustine, Fr, O.F.M.Cap.: *Footprints of Father Mathew*. (Dublin 1947).

Booth, C.,: An article in Coyne's *Ireland, Industrial and Agricultural* (Dublin 1901) entitled *Economic Distribution of Population*.

Chart, G. D. A.,: *Unskilled Labour in Dublin*. (Dublin 1914).

Connolly, James: *Socialism and Nationalism*. (Dublin 1948 edition). *The Workers' Republic*. (Dublin 1951 edition, ed. Desmond Ryan).

Cooke, James: Evidence given by him as Hon Treasurer of the N.S.P.C.C. at *Government Enquiry into Dublin Housing Conditions*. (Dublin 1913).

Cosgrave, Dillon: *North Dublin City and Environs*. (Dublin 1909).

Cosgrave, E.: *Dictionary of Dublin*. (Dublin 1908).

Cullen, Paul, Cardinal: Pastorals and writings in the Dublin Diocesan Archives.

Donnelly, N. Revd Dr,:*History of the Dublin Parishes*. (Dublin 1907).

Fingall, Countess of,: *Seventy Years Young*. (London 1937).

Fitzpatrick, W. J.,: *Father Burke, O.P.* (2 volumes London 1885). *History of the Dublin Catholic Cemeteries.* (Dublin 1900).

Fleetwood, Dr John,: *History of Medicine in Ireland.* (Dublin 1951).

Gerard, Frances: *Picturesque Dublin, Old and New.* (London 1898).

Gibbons, Margaret: *Life of Margaret Aylward.* (London 1928).

Glynn, Sir Joseph: *Life of Matt Talbot, a Dublin Labourer.* (Dublin 1925). *Life of Matt Talbot.* (Dublin 1928).

Horgan, John J.,: *Parnell to Pearse* (Dublin 1948).

I.T. & G.W. Union: *The attempt to smash the I.T.G.W.U.* (Dublin 1924).

Marjoribanks, Edward: *Life of Lord Carson.* (2 vols London 1932).

Moran, Patrick: *Writings of Cardinal Cullen:* (3 vols Dublin 1882).

O'Farrell, Seumas: *The Changing Pattern of Irish Life* (article in *Studies,* Dublin 1951).

O'Riordan, Rev. M.,: *Catholicity and Progress in Ireland.* (St Louis, 1906).

Perraud, l'Abbé: *Etudes sur l'Irlande contemporaine.* (Paris 1862).

Quigley, Canon E.,: *His Eminence and His Grace,* a series of articles in the *Irish Ecclesiastical Record* (Dublin 1925-1926).

Rogers, Patrick: *Father Theobald Mathew.* (Dublin 1943).

Ronan, Dr Myles V.,: *An Apostle of Catholic Dublin* (Dublin 1944).

Ryan, W. P.,: *The Irish Labour Movement.* (Dublin 1919).

Sullivan, A. M.: *New Ireland.* (London 1877).

Thackeray, W. M.,: *The Irish Sketch-Book.* (London 1843).

Webb, J.J.: *Industrial Dublin since 1698.* (Dublin and London 1913).

Willis, Thomas: *Conditions in the North Dublin Union* an article in the *Dublin Journal of Medical Science* (Dublin 1845 May).

Wright, Arnold: *Disturbed Dublin.* (London 1914).

Other Biographies

Carroll, Malachy Gerard: *The Story of Matt Talbot.* 118 pages. (Cork, Ireland, 1948).

Doherty, Eddie: *Matt Talbot.* 200 pages. (Milwaukee, 1953).

Dolan, Albert H.: *Matt Talbot, Alcoholic.* 47 pages. (Chicago, 1947). *We Knew Matt Talbot.* 129 pages. (Chicago, 1948).

Golland Trindade, Dom Frei Henrique: *Matt Talbot, Worker and Penitent: His Life as Seen through Franciscan Eyes.* Translated from the Portuguese by Conall Leary. 126 pages. (Paterson, N.J., 1953).

Wedge, Florence: *The Thirst of Matt Talbot.* 48 pages. (Pulaski, Wisconsin, 1967).

Venerable Matt Talbot (1856-1925), Champion against Alcoholism, four-page leaflet with approved prayer for Matt's beatification and canonization, available from Franciscan Herald Press, 1434 W. 51st St., Chicago, IL 60609.